How The Letters Dance Me

How The Letters Dance Me

Guidebook for the Vimala Alphabet®

Jennifer Crebbin

Heart Wisdom Publishing
2015

Cover design by Maxima Kahn | Editing by Lauren Forcella | Graphic design by Teddi Jensen

Heart Wisdom Publishing P.O. Box 1803 Nevada City, CA 95959
ISBN-13:978-0-692-411110-0 ISBN-10:0-692-41110-0

Also by Jennifer Crebbin:
Soul Development through Handwriting: The Waldorf Approach to the Vimala Alphabet®
published by SteinerBooks

Thank you to Vimala Rodgers for creating the inspirational Vimala Alphabet®.

www.ChangeYourHandwriting.com

Forward

As of this writing, 41 U.S. states have adopted the Common Core State Standards for English which have deleted cursive from their requirements. Think about that. A multi-thousand-year-old practice hacked down in one generation in favor of keyboarding. We've bitten the "Apple" in what's left of the Garden of Childhood (or perhaps your school has taken "Windows" to Nowhere). Many high school students and young adults today not only can't write in cursive, they can't read it either, as infamously demonstrated in the Trayvon Martin murder trial, when the star witness, a rising public-school senior, was unable to read a single word of her own dictation taken in cursive.

So what's so great about cursive? Learning cursive is akin to learning a musical instrument in the profound neurological benefits it imparts. For the juvenile brain, technology stunts growth, whereas complex hand-brain activities such as playing a musical instrument and writing in cursive, boost brain development like powerful fertilizers. Brain scanning and other extensive research show that cursive writing co-activates multiple areas of the brain (that keyboarding and block printing do not). The task of joining flowing curving forms into meaningful words integrates sensation, motor control and executive thinking — things vital for reading, memory and composing thoughts and ideas.

My youngest son, now 23, recalled his first day of first grade. It was a Waldorf classroom of about 24 students and the teacher drew a lemniscate on the blackboard (a sideways figure-eight) and asked the children to draw it on their own paper. Much to his amazement, not a single child was able to do it. In other words, drawing flowing looping forms is difficult! Our children need this challenge for much more than the skill of written communication. Tapping keys is fundamentally easy, as is block printing. Cursive is not. It truly exercises, tasks and demands integration of different regions of the brain like no other grade-school exercise. It also requires and builds focus and concentration, a growing childhood deficit in need of a remedy. In addition, cursive has long been an early-detection tool for learning disorders and is used to correct dyslexia. Teachers report a sense of peace in the classroom when children are practicing cursive — another added benefit in a world speeding out of control. The pen is indeed mighty, in more ways than we realize.

Most children don't have the privilege to afford a musical instrument, much less music lessons, but just a few short years ago, children didn't need to be privileged to get their 45 minutes of cursive practice per day, spanning multiple years. Now, unless you are at certain private schools — or very lucky — even schools that do teach cursive, spend only 5-15 minutes per day, and usually for only one year.

The Vimala cursive forms have arrived on the scene like a medic in a MASH unit. While cursive is "laid up," waiting for what I hope will be a full recovery back into childhood education, it's the perfect time to reset a few bones. Since cursive itself helps the brain grow and integrate, it makes sense to feed the brain optimum cursive forms. Form reflects being. The outer form in which we sit, stand and move, reflects our interior psycho-emotional state. The form of our handwriting mirrors it as well — leaving, literally, a written record for those who know how to read it. Psychologists know that these processes work in reverse, too, and by changing our outer forms, we can't help but change inside in response.

The Vimala letters meet today's challenging times with cursive forms that support evolutionary human qualities: engaged interaction, clarity, honesty, boundaries, perspective, gratitude, openness, focus, conflict resolution, completion, discernment, creativity, love, care, connection. These are just some of the qualities that the different letters of the Vimala Alphabet® bring — as you will see by turning the pages.

It's an honor to write the forward for this guidebook. Not only am I an advocate for cursive instruction in schools using the Vimala script, I, myself, practice the Vimala forms. I was fortunate to learn cursive as a child as well and do recall the peaceful feeling in the classroom while we were practicing. I found that peace and clarity again during my digital-free Vimala practice time and I also experienced mental and psychological benefits as my handwriting shifted into these consciously-derived forms.

Whether you are a child, teacher, seeker or wizard, you will receive many benefits from the rich and complex human practice of speaking words through conscious handwriting. Without further ado, may I introduce to you the Vimala letters — they will indeed dance you!

—Lauren Forcella, Founder & Editor, Straight Talk Advice.org
March 19, 2015

Table of Contents

Introduction

For me, the letters of the alphabet flow and move across the page like a dance. In life, I have my dance and you have yours. Each of us dances a bit differently, naturally reflecting our diverse backgrounds and roles. Together we make the dance of life wonderful, each playing a richly individual and important part.

Each unique dance of life is recorded on paper through our handwriting. Every single day, as we walk, talk, eat, breathe, sing, share, work and create our way through life — sometimes with awareness and sometimes without — the dance of our handwriting captures the dance of our life. It captures our hesitations, doubts and fears, as well as our joys, talents and desires. These qualities are in our handwriting for anyone to see who knows how to read this dance.

Life happens. There can be joyful times and there can be times of suffering, numbness or feeling stuck. Through the tumult, we can sometimes forget that we have a vital role in the dance of life, each having a special piece needed by the whole. Sometimes we lose trust, forget our connection and feel lost. All this shows up in our writing as blocks or obstacles.

The good news is these obstacles can be removed from our life by removing them from our handwriting. When we move differently, our life changes. When we write differently, our life changes as well. "Insanity," said Albert Einstein, "is doing the same thing over and over again and expecting different results." In other words, if we are always moving or writing the same way, we cannot expect our lives to change. When we change, life changes with us!

I help people overcome obstacles by changing their handwriting. The pages that follow detail the alphabetical forms that bring flow and ease into life. The practice of writing these forms helps us become more of who we truly are, who we came into this world to be. They help us dance our individual dance as it was intended, with beauty, grace and style.

The forms shown here are from the Vimala Alphabet®, created by Vimala Rodgers. These alphabetical forms support the transforming, awakening and developing of capacities buried inside us. They help us realize our full potential and live joy-filled lives. The description of the letters, their movements and meaning are distilled from many years of working with these letters and helping others do the same. This is how the letters dance me.

Please join me in exploring these beautiful forms and receiving the gifts they bring!

How To Practice The Vimala Alphabet®

The thing that will help you the most in your practice of the Vimala Alphabet® is unconditional friendliness toward yourself. This is no place for belittling yourself, or practicing shame or guilt. If such thoughts arise, put your pen down, center yourself in loving kindness and begin again. Speak to yourself as you would a small child trying to master a new task. Practice being loving, present and positive. It makes a world of difference!

It is very helpful to sit at a desk with feet flat on the ground with your knees slightly higher than your hip bones. Your arms should rest on the table with your spine erect. This position will support you in sitting comfortably and enable you to write without strain.

Grasp your pen with your thumb, index and middle fingers. Ideally, you will have the tips of all three of these fingers pressing against the pen. You could also place the pen between your index and middle finger if that allows the fingertips to more easily press into the pen.

This book includes several different practice sheets. There is everything from beginner's practice sheets with dotted lines to sheets that assist in deep integration of the forms. You can choose what speaks to you. Copy the practice pages from this book to write on and keep the originals clean to create more pages later.

Writing the exact forms is important, especially in the beginning. It is like learning ballet or a musical instrument. First you learn the basics, then, once you have some mastery, your own style, something uniquely "you" arises without effort. No two people dance Swan Lake exactly alike and so it is with writing. Even striving to write the Vimala Alphabet® identically, no two people ever write it the same. We are each unique and irreplaceable. That is how the dance of life is!

The practice pages for each letter include:

- Large letters for tracing with your finger or pen
- Step-by-step instructions showing the path of each stroke
- Dotted lines to practice uppercase and lowercase letters together
- Line guides for size and zones occupied by each letter
- Pages for practicing both letters and words that contain the letter

The most integrative practice is to write three rows of uppercase and lowercase letters, followed by three rows of words that contain the letter, one row *beginning* with the letter, one row *containing* the letter, and one row *ending* with the letter. Many have told me that thinking of these words is part of the fun!

In addition, you will find a blank practice guide for zone and slant. Please use the zone and slant guide only until you are able to make the letters properly on your own.

Line guides can become crutches. If we break our leg, we only use crutches to help us until we're strong enough to move on our own. The same goes for the line guides; they are learning aids only. It is vital that you integrate these letters into your being and be able to form them out of your own forces, independent of outside assistance.

To help you select which letters to practice, see the "Index of Human Qualities and the Corresponding Letter," at the back of this book. Here you will find additional practice tips and considerations.

I have received many requests for a book covering the fine-detail specifications on how to draw each of the Vimala Alphabet® forms and how to choose letters to practice. This guidebook is my response to these requests. I hope it is helpful for everyone, from child to teacher, and beginning and advanced student alike. Enjoy!

Zones and Slant Lines

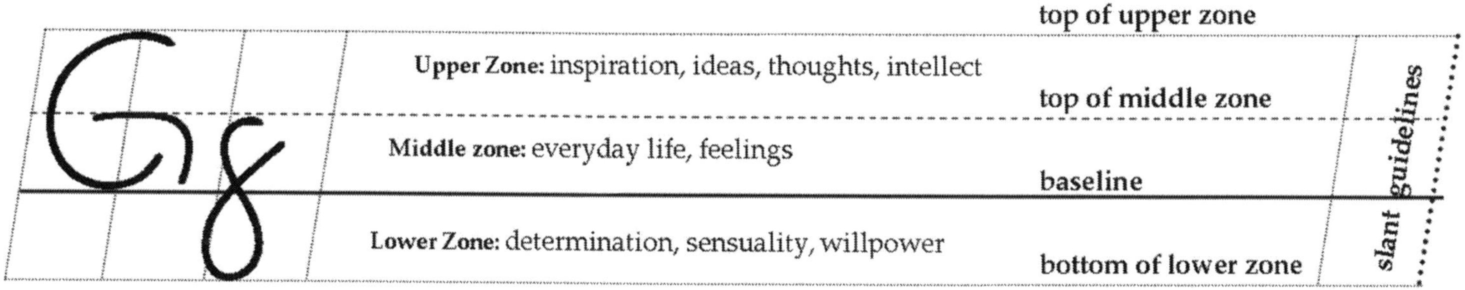

This key above shows the zones and what they represent, as well as the ideal 5-degree slant line for the letters.

Zones: When we make a loop and bring the tail into the middle zone, we are capturing the energy of that zone and bringing it to work in our lives. For example, in the lowercase g, the loop in the lower zone brings our gratitude into action when we bring the end of the loop into the middle zone.

Slant: This is the way the letter sits on the baseline. Does it lean to the right, stand upright or lean to the left? A slight lean to the right of 5-degrees is desirable. In the back of this guidebook there is a line guide showing zone and slant so you can practice the desired slant.

An Alphabet That Leads To Love

by Hubert McFarland

I am an articulate alchemist
ameliorating axioms about
Beings becoming bridges
bounding bigotry
Compassionately consciously
conserving continual consciousness
Denouncing dependencies diligently
defending diversities
Earnestly emitting encouragements
embodying empowerment
Fearlessly fostering forgiveness
fortifying foundations for freedom
Germinating gentle governance
graciously garnering goodwill
Honestly helping humankind
harbor humility
Insightfully instituting impunities
irrevocably instilled
Judiciously joining Jesus'
joyous journey
Knowing kindheartedness
knits kaleidoscopic kindred ships
Learning life's lessons
leaving limitless love
Masterfully manipulating
muscle-maximizing movement
Nurturing nature and neighbors
never negating
Objectively obliterating obscenities
overcoming ostracisms
Producing plethora of
positive purposeful poetry
Questing quasi quietly
queuing quality quotes
Romancing rhymes realizing
rewards rarely received

Sharing stored away secrets
savoring scintillating skin
Teaching that thoughtful touch
transfers trust
Understanding universal unity
ultimately unlocks utopia
Vocalizing virtuous vibrations
vertically vitalizing
Working words wondrously
wanting to wander worldwide
Exceptions will be made for the letter X
exceptions should be made in life
I experience ecstasy by giving extra
Yielding yin and yang
yet yearning for you all
This brings us to the letter Z
the alphabet's end
But the letter Z
should not end our ability to communicate
For with zeal we should zestfully seek
to unite zillions across the globe because
Love knows no zip code

The Letters

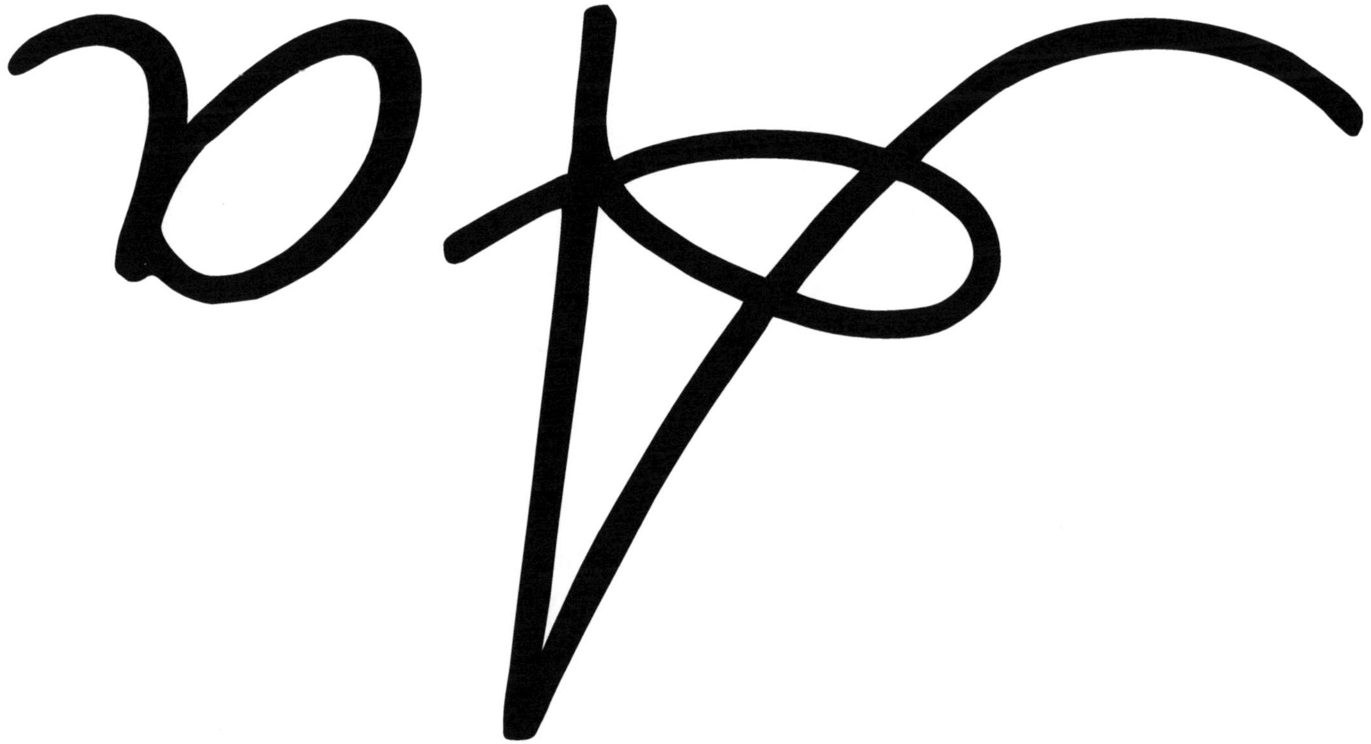

Aa

The letter A speaks of a continuum of self-acceptance and confidence, especially in relationship to our bodies.

This letter leads us to:
I accept all parts of myself, just as I am.

To form this letter:

A Beginning slightly above baseline, dip down to the baseline then up with a sweeping stroke to the top of the upper zone. From there, an "I am" stroke follows, coming down at a 5-degree slant to the baseline. Without lifting your pen, head up and to the left, forming a loop called a tie stroke or perseverance stroke.

a Starting at the top of the middle zone, form a small oval in the middle zone making sure you close the oval at the top. From there, bring the stroke down to the baseline and reach out with a garland. This garland is a little cup or hand reaching out to join the next letter in a gesture of connection and friendliness.

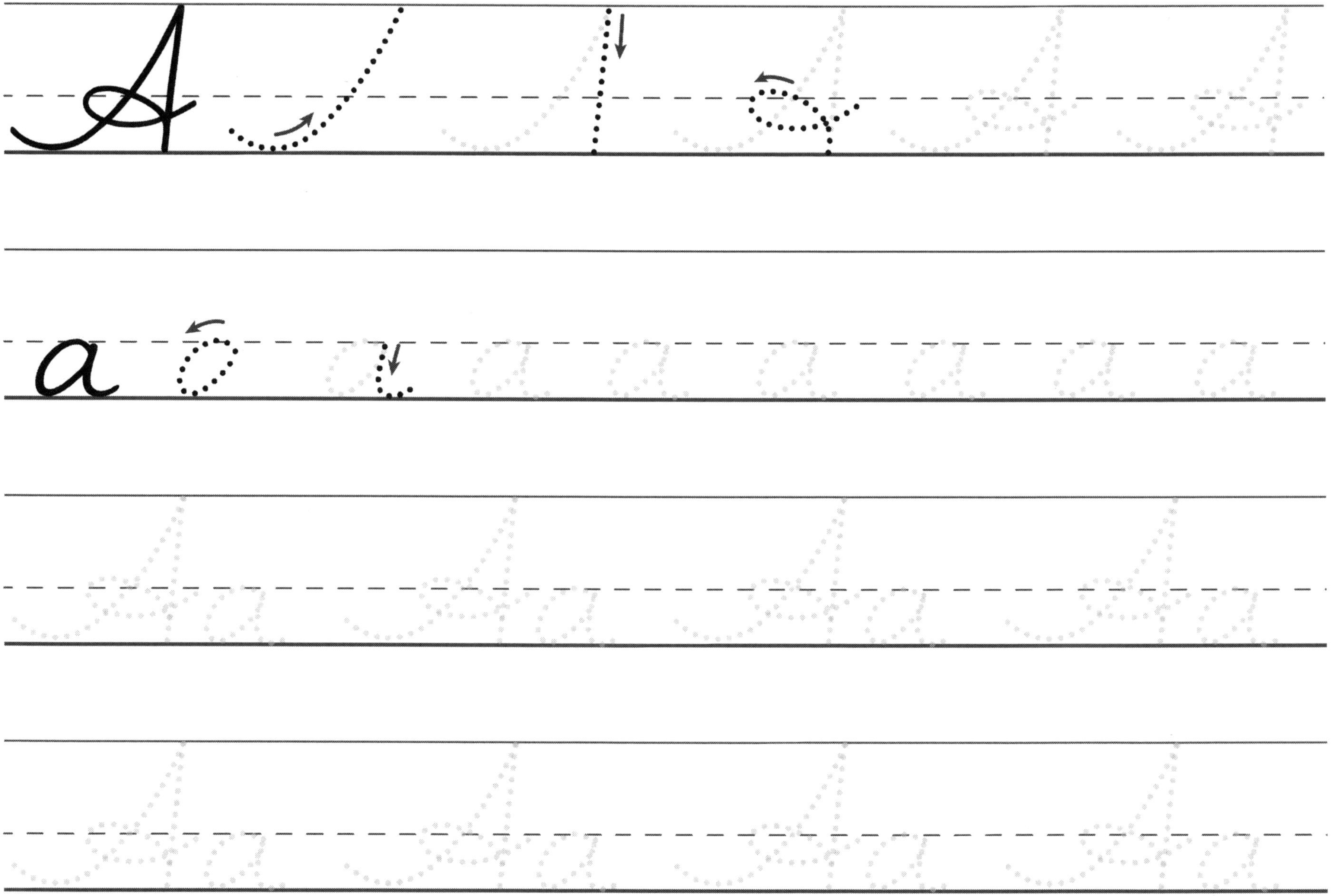

Aa

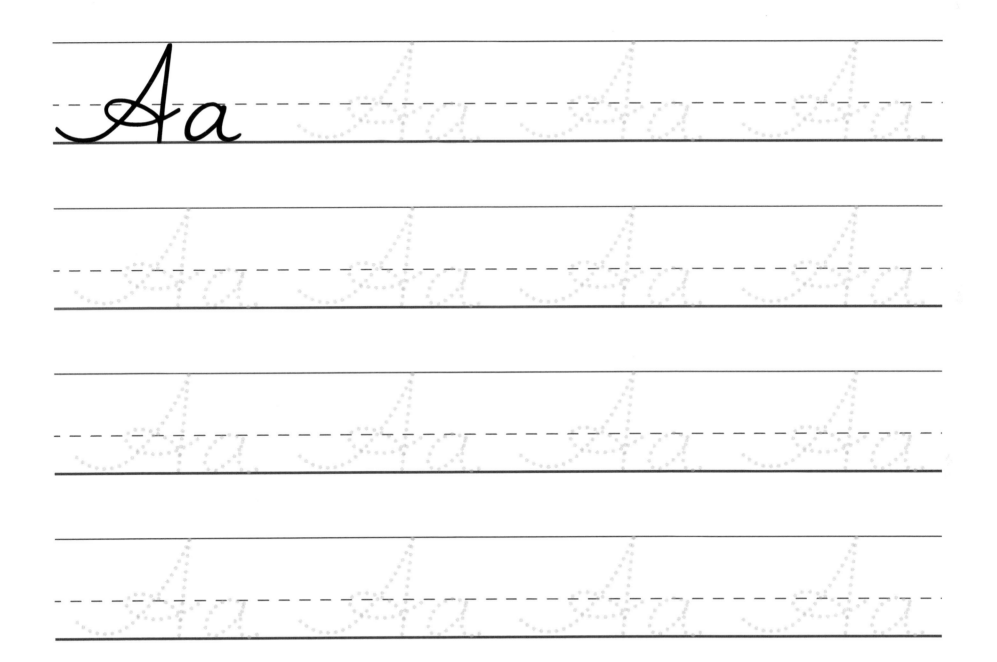

Aa

Fill in each row and complete the page with writing.

Aa

Aa

Aa

Acε

wag

yεa

Bb

The letter B addresses our relationship to community and generosity.

This letter leads us to:
I am working for the highest good of all.

To form this letter:

B Begin at the tiptop of the upper zone with an "I am" stroke, gathering the gifts from heaven and bringing them down to manifestation on earth. The second stroke starts just to the left of or at the top of the "I am" stroke and forms two stacked backward "c" shapes. Note, the top "c" is the smaller and there is no loop between them. Be sure to touch the "I am" stroke in the middle of the two "c" shapes (ignore what is shown in the font) and at the baseline. This letter ends with the prayer gesture, reaching out in gratitude to share blessings with the community.

b Start with the "I am" stroke, then lift your pen about a third of the way back up the stroke to begin a rounded backward "c" that touches the "I am" stroke and comes forward with the prayer gesture in an attitude of gratitude and sharing.

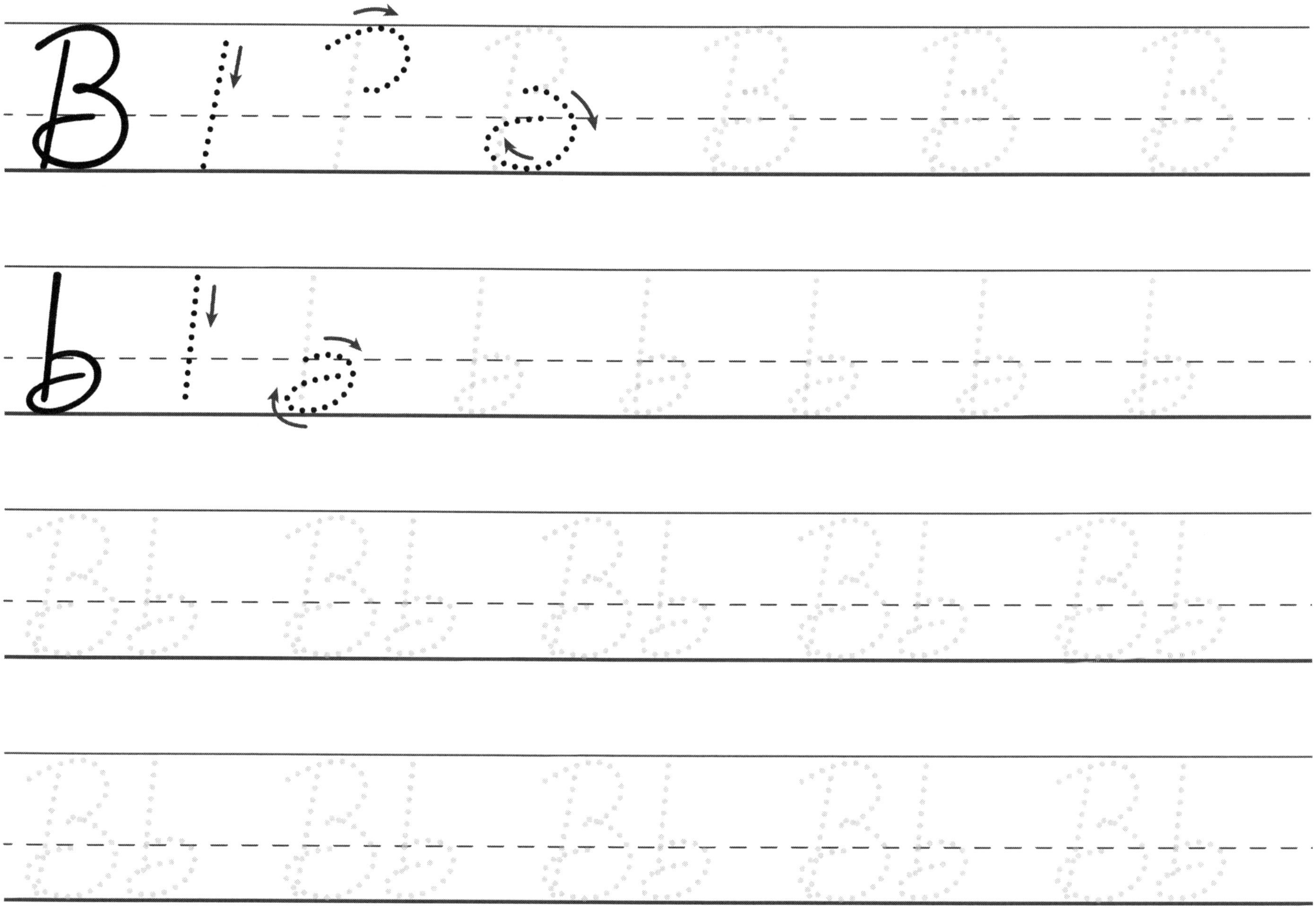

Bb

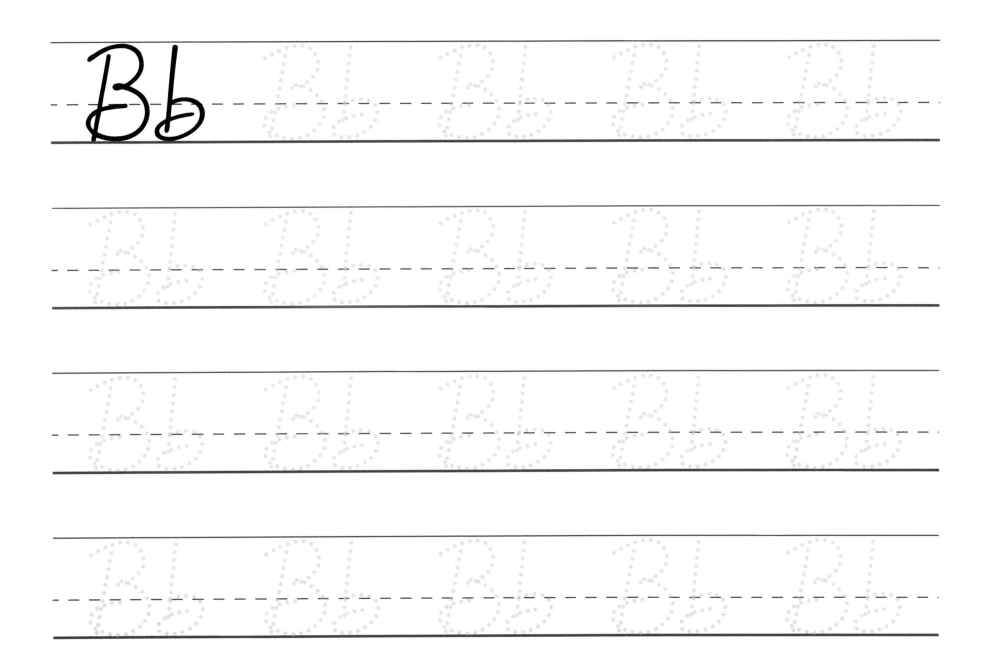

Bb

Fill in each row and complete the page with writing.

Bb

Bb

Bb

Build

ibis

bulb

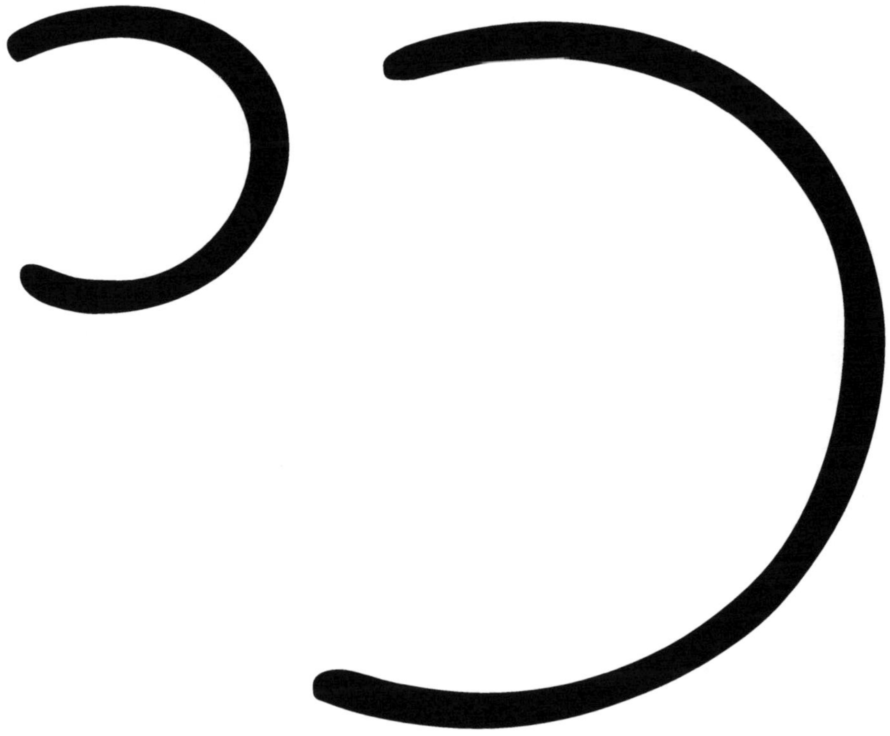

Cc

To form this letter:

C Place your pen slightly below the top of the upper zone. In one smooth line, make a complete arc that touches both the top of the upper zone and the baseline and ends inside the middle zone slightly above baseline. Though it has no hooks or loops, this very simple form is extremely challenging to make.

c The lowercase letter is formed exactly the same as its uppercase companion only is entirely within the middle zone.

The letter C guides us in trusting and surrendering to the support of The Infinite.

This letter leads us to:
I am supported and held by The Divine.

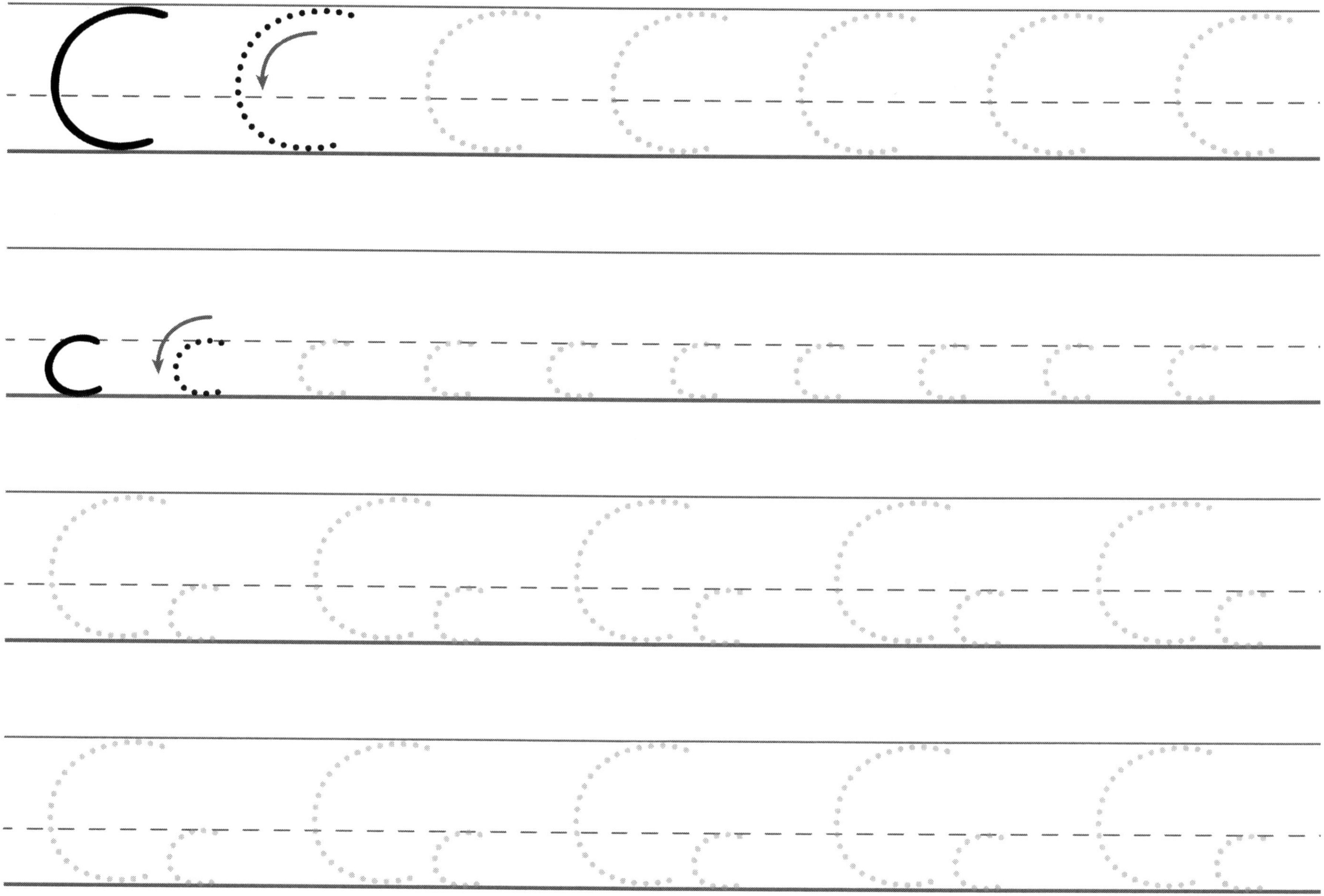

Cc

Cc

Fill in each row and complete the page with writing.

Cc

Cc

Cc

Caring

nice

music

Dd

The letter D reflects one's sense of identity and teaches boundaries, self-reliance and skill in handling conflict.

This letter leads us to:
I am strong in myself. I see every act as an act of love or a request for love.

To form this letter:

D Begin with an "I am" stroke. The second stroke starts either at the top of the "I am" stroke or slightly to the left of it and forms an expansive backward "c" shape that meets the "I am" stroke again at the baseline. From here it comes forward with a prayer stroke, a gesture reaching out to join the next letter. This is not a slim letter, be sure to make it wide.

d Start at the top of the middle zone and form a closed oval. From here, bring the stem up at a 5-degree slant to the very top of the upper zone. Then, retrace the stem back down to the baseline without forming a loop in the stem and end with a little garland, like a hand reaching out to join the next letter. The lowercase Vimala d is every bit as tall as any uppercase letter.

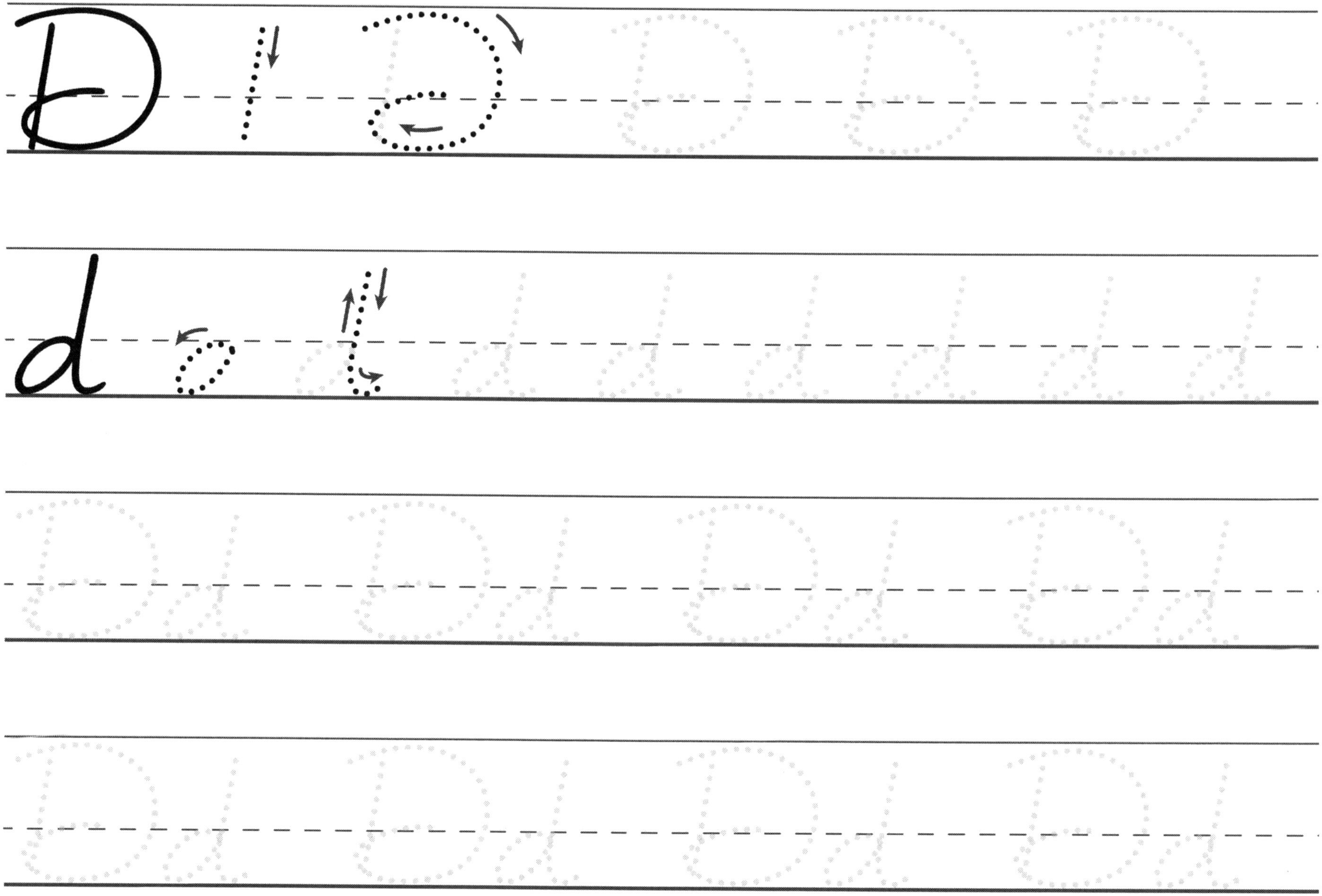

Dd

Dd

Fill in each row and complete the page with writing.

Dd

Dd

Dd

Divine

radio

aid

з З

E e e

To form this letter:

- E Start just below the top of the upper zone forming two sideways "u" shapes, stacked one atop the other, the top "u" being slightly smaller. Very importantly, there is no loop between the two "u" shapes.
- e The lowercase letter is formed the same as the uppercase except it occupies only the middle zone.
- e For this alternate form of the lowercase e, be sure to begin and end on the baseline making a full loop in the middle zone.

The letter E teaches tolerance and acceptance of self, others and the world.

This letter leads us to:
I love and accept the world and myself as we exist in the present moment, knowing that how I see the world is a reflection of how I see myself.

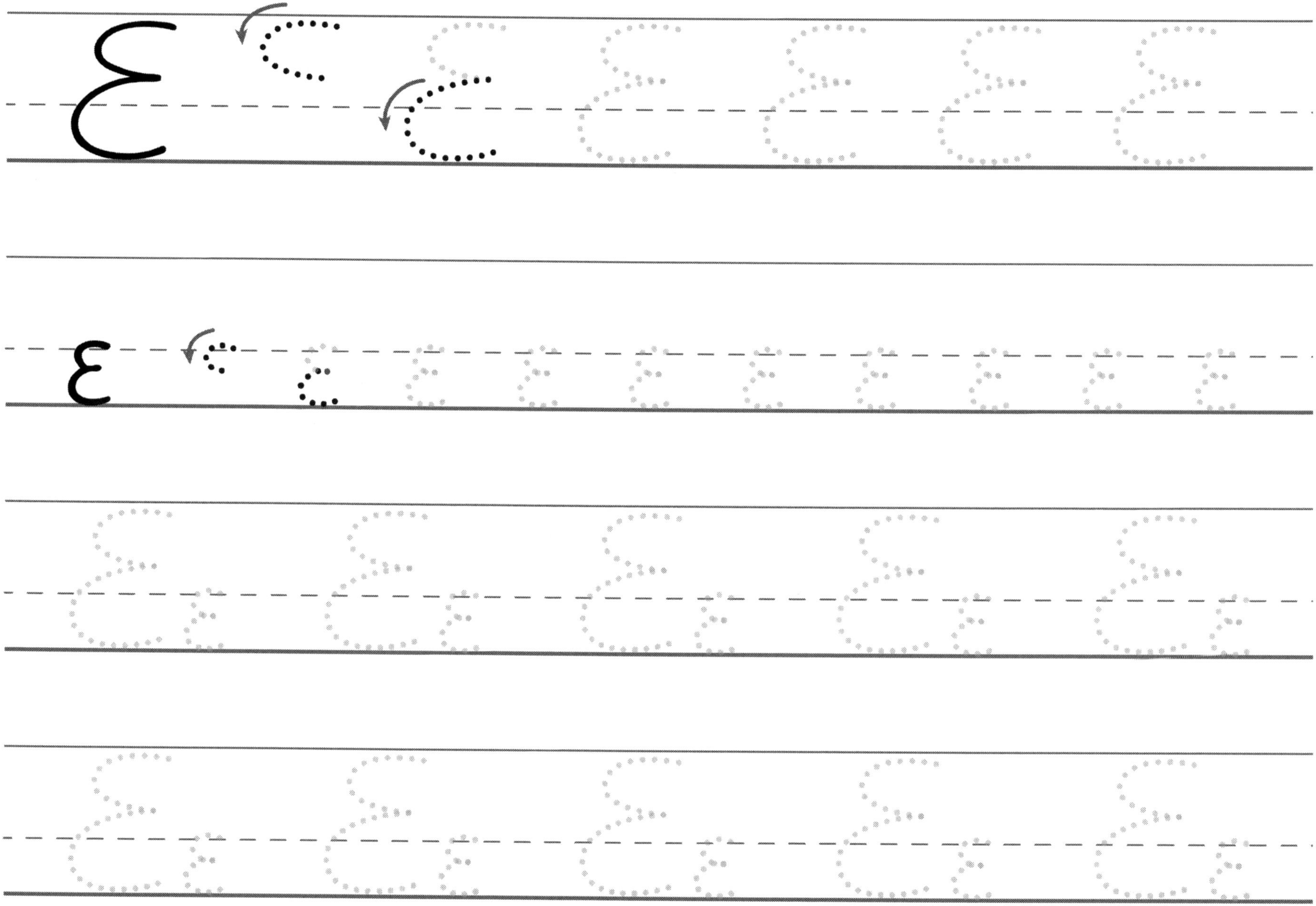

Ɛɛ

Ee

Fill in each row and complete the page with writing.

Ee

Ee

Ee

Excel

insert

here

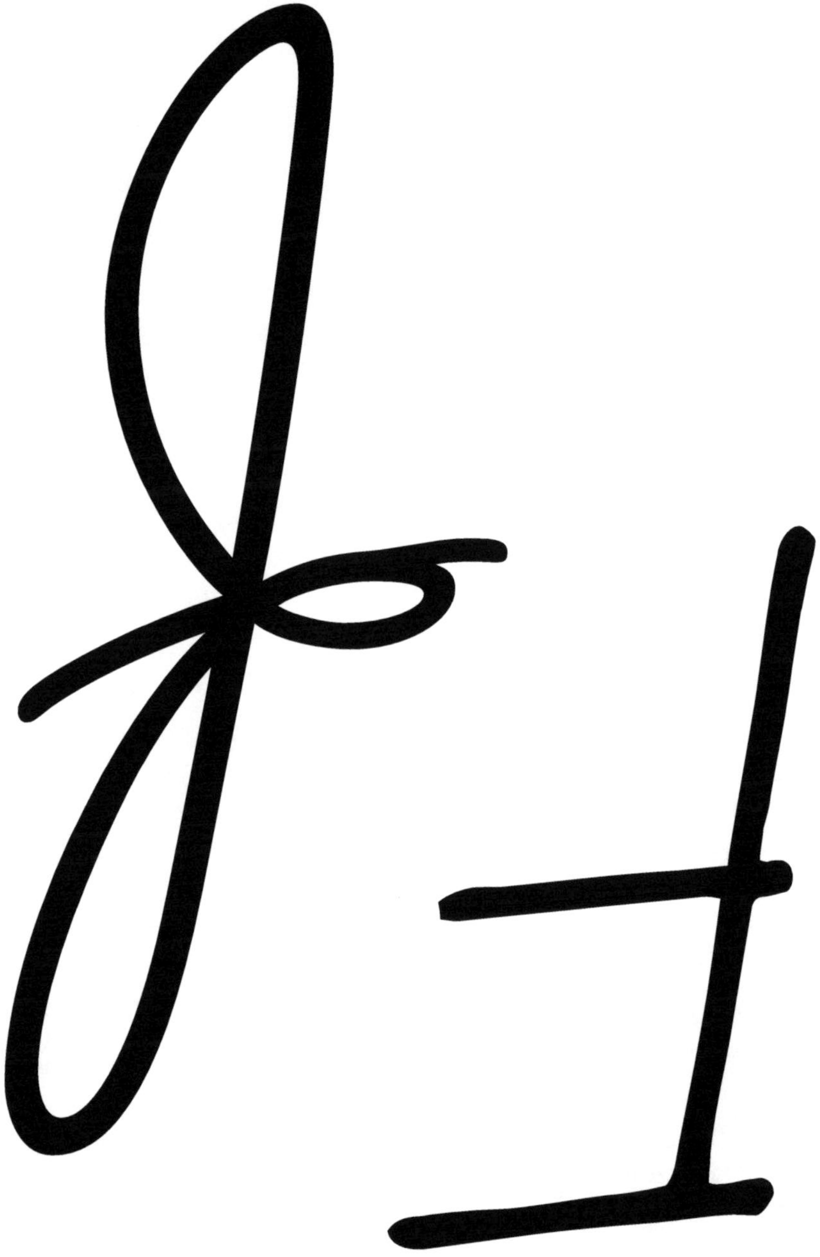

The letter F is about creatively sharing our work with the world.

This letter leads us to:
I engage my creativity with tenacity.

To form this letter:

F Start with the "I am" stroke. The second stroke starts at the top of the "I am" stroke and goes to the right, if anything, slanting slightly upward. The third stroke starts at the "I am" stroke in the upper zone and also heads to the right parallel to the second stroke.

f Begin at baseline with a little garland. Then climb to the very top of the upper zone, making a loop which gathers creativity, insight and inspiration from the heavens. From the top of that loop, come down with a straight 5-degree slanted line all the way to the bottom of the lower zone. This straight line is the backbone of the letter. At the bottom of the lower zone, make another loop which says, "I am in action with the ideas and creative gifts gathered above." When returning to baseline from the lower loop, go across the backbone to the left, forming the tie stroke. The tie stroke is the hardest part and is entirely to the left of the backbone stroke. The completed tie stroke then heads across the backbone stroke to the right saying, "I trust in the outcome. I place the results in God's/Spirit's hands."

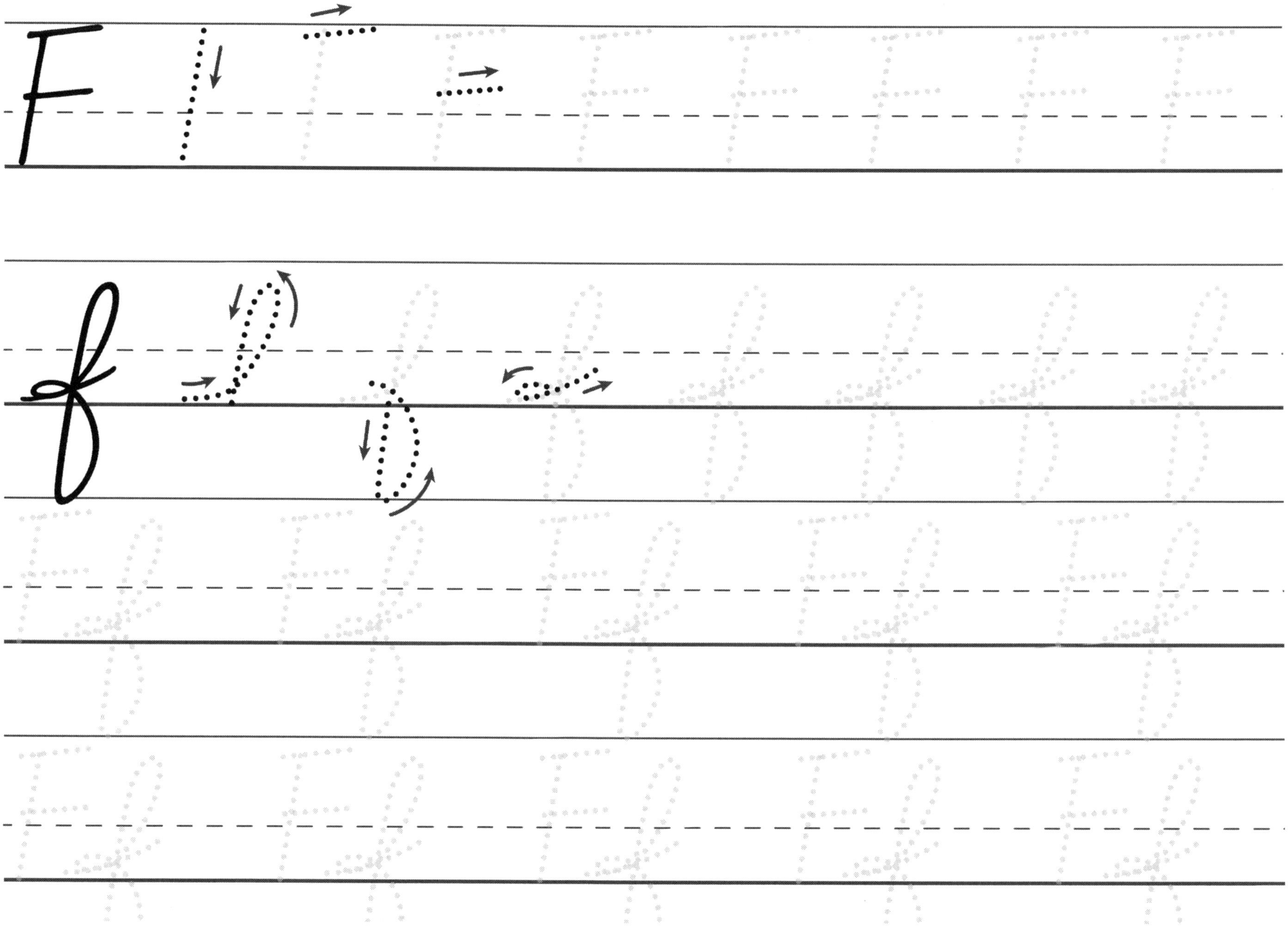

Ff

Ff

Fill in each row and complete the page with writing.

Ff

Ff

Ff

Fun

craft

chef

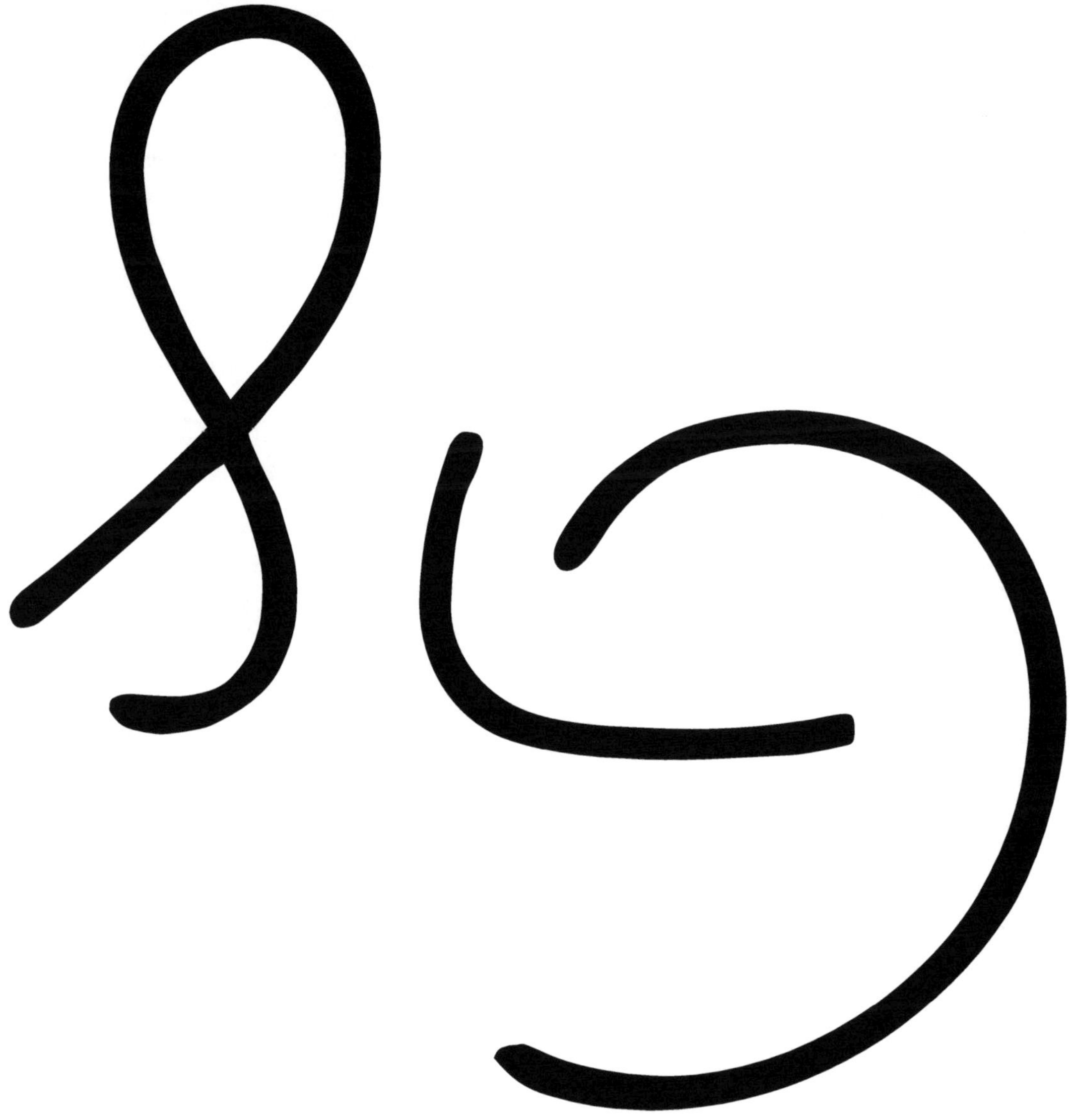

The letter G helps with focus, task completion, working with others, and gratitude.

This letter leads us to:
I am grateful and I express it.

To form this letter:

 Start with a Vimala C, imbuing it with C's knowingness that all is perfect, we are provided for and cared for. This letter has no angles, just soft, curvy heart energy. The second stroke does not connect to the first stroke at any point. It starts deep inside the "c" shape heading to the right parallel to baseline, then, with a very gentle curve turns downward to end on the baseline. It must end in the middle zone, not dip into the lower zone, so this flow can manifest in everyday life.

 Begin at the top of the middle zone with a slight "c" shape in the middle zone, and then drop down into the lower zone forming a beautiful loop. You want to feel the weight in the bottom of this loop, creating a container in the lower zone. Bring this energy back to the middle zone and harness it for use in everyday life.

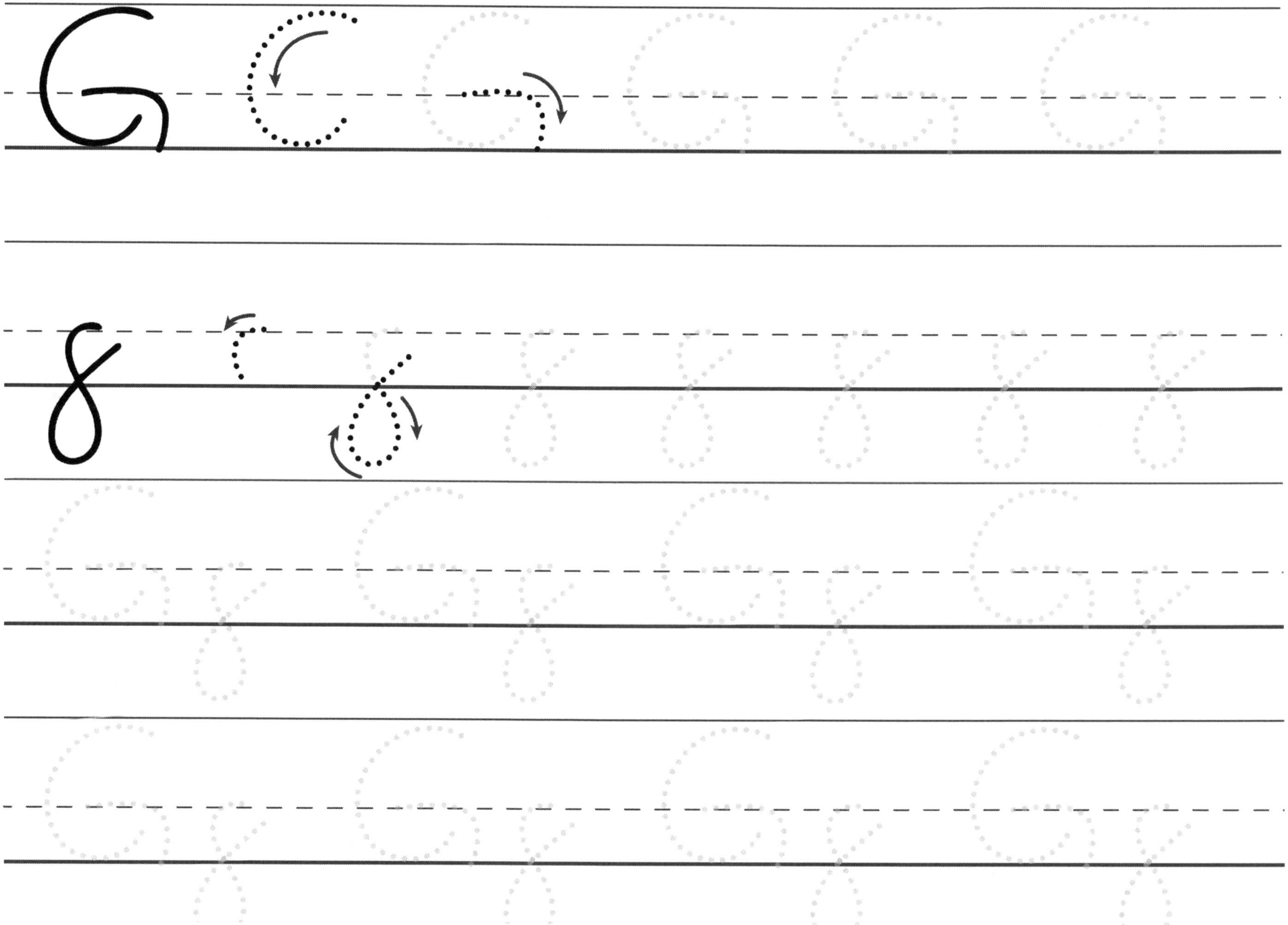

Gg

Gg

Fill in each row and complete the page with writing.

Gg

Gg

Gg

Grace

again

sing

YAH

Hh

The letter H lets us stand with confidence in who we are and what we know.

This letter leads us to:
I stand solidly in my life as a pure reflection of The Divine.

To form this letter:

H Starting at the top of the upper zone, gathering the gifts from heaven, we proceed to baseline with the first "I am" stroke. If this first "I am" was not clear enough, it repeats itself with a second "I am." And if that was not enough, without lifting our pen from the bottom of the second "I am" stroke, we form a large tie stroke saying, "I am persistent."

h Starting at baseline, form a very tall, full loop in an "l" shape that reaches to the top of the upper zone, returning with a 5-degree slant stroke to baseline. From here, form a narrow "v" before the arcade in the middle zone. Once this arcade reaches the top of the middle zone, it returns to baseline in a full and expansive manner, either straight down or to the right, never cramping itself the slightest bit to the left.

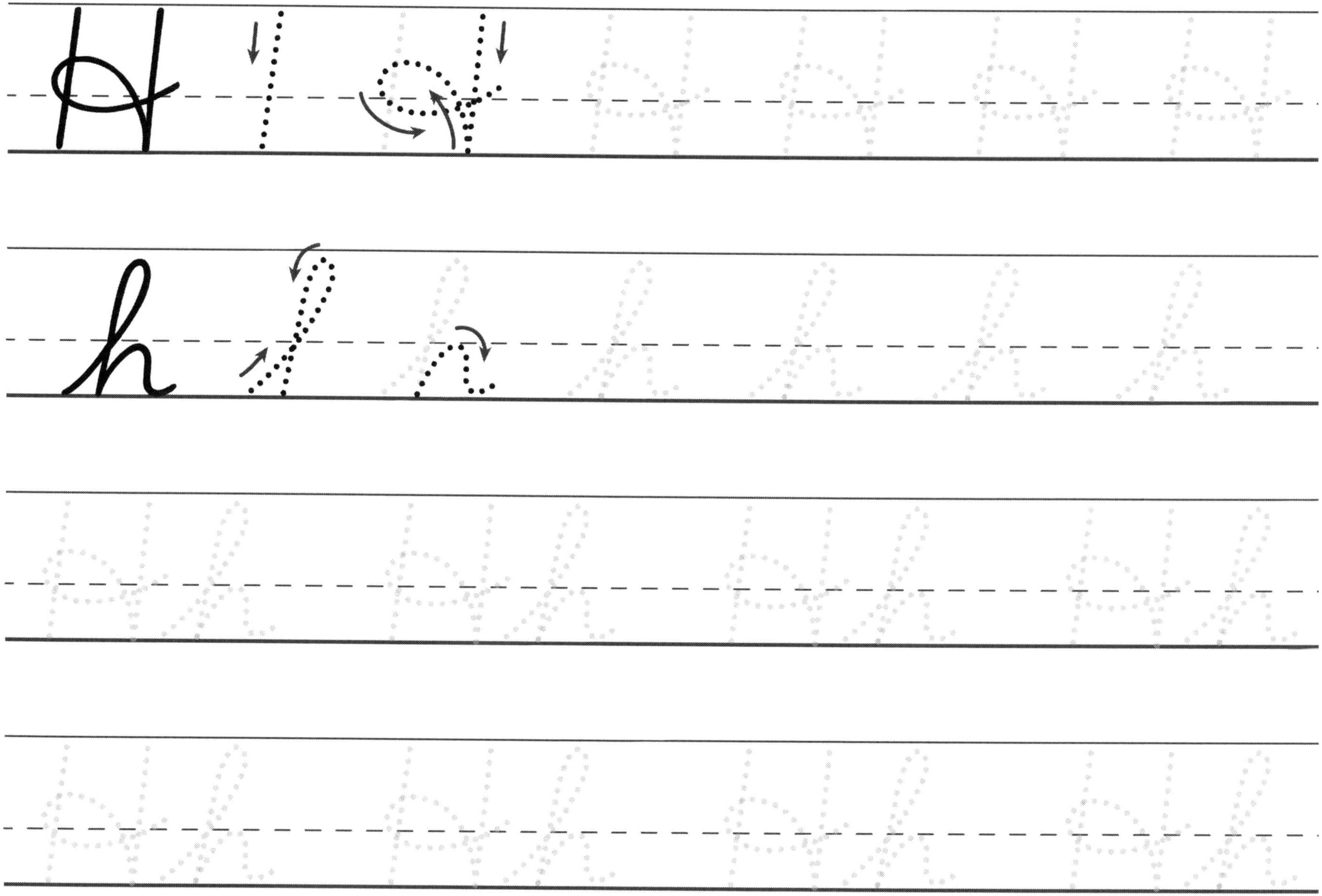

Hh

Hh

Fill in each row and complete the page with writing.

Hh

Hh

Hh

Honor

achieve

health

?I

Ii

The letter I helps us gain clear perspective and understanding of the world.

This letter leads us to:
With clarity, I see the world as it is.

To form this letter:

I — Begin with the "I am" stroke from the top of the upper zone to the baseline. The next stroke, at the top of the "I am," goes from left to right with the right side highest. The lower stroke, goes from left to right along the baseline. Make sure both crossbars are centered evenly on the stem.

i — Beginning at the baseline, go to the top of the middle zone at a 5-degree slant, then retrace the stem back down to the baseline and reach out to the next letter with a friendly garland. A dot is placed just above the stem.

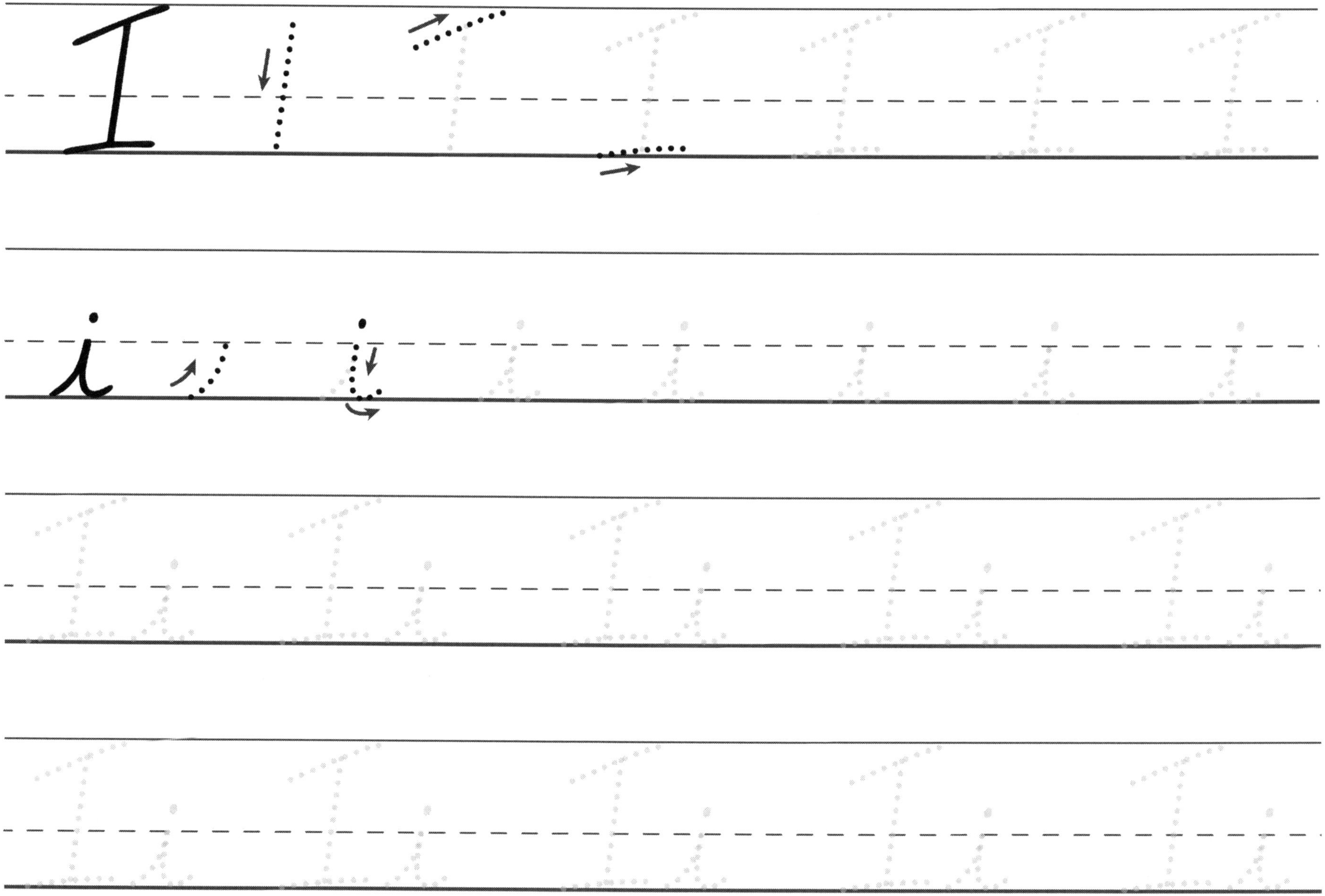

Ii

Ii

Fill in each row and complete the page with writing.

Ii

Ii

Ii

Insight

risk

koi

The letter J brings us intuition and insight.

This letter leads us to:
I trust my inner guidance.

To form this letter:

J Starting just below baseline, form a large upper loop. Then, come down with the 5-degree slant to the bottom of the lower zone, where you will form another loop to the left. As the lower loop returns to baseline, it crosses over the down stroke, forming a small sideways "v" at the baseline where the beginning and ending strokes cross.

j Begin at the baseline with a small garland that arcs up to the top of the middle zone. From there, the letter heads back down, continuing into the lower zone at a 5-degree slant. A loop is formed to the left in the lower zone returning to end in the middle zone. A dot is placed just above the stem.

Jj

Jj

Fill in each row and complete the page with writing.

Jj

Jj

Jj

Jump

rejoice

Taj

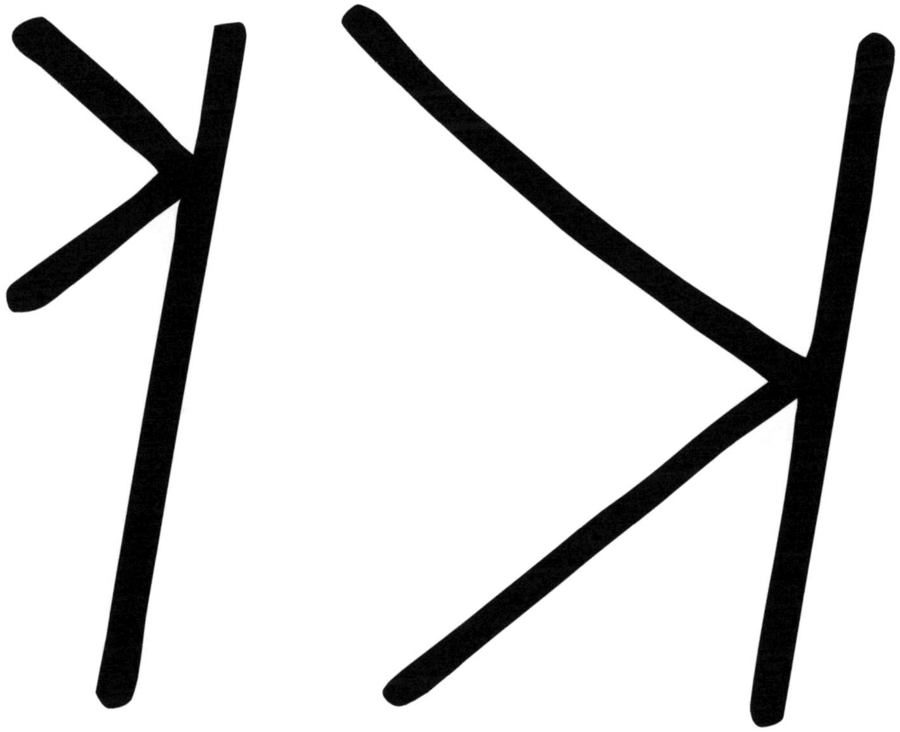

Kk

To form this letter:

K Start at the top of the upper zone with an "I am" stroke. The second stroke also starts at the top of the upper zone to the right of the first stroke and angles sharply into the "I am" stroke at the top of the middle zone, then vees back out to the right again, ending at baseline. There are absolutely no curves in the K.

k Start at the top of the upper zone with an "I am" stroke. The second stroke forms a small sideways "v" that occupies only the middle zone.

The letter K helps us to own our power, not be fearful of it or give it away.

This letter leads us to:
I now take the action needed in the moment.

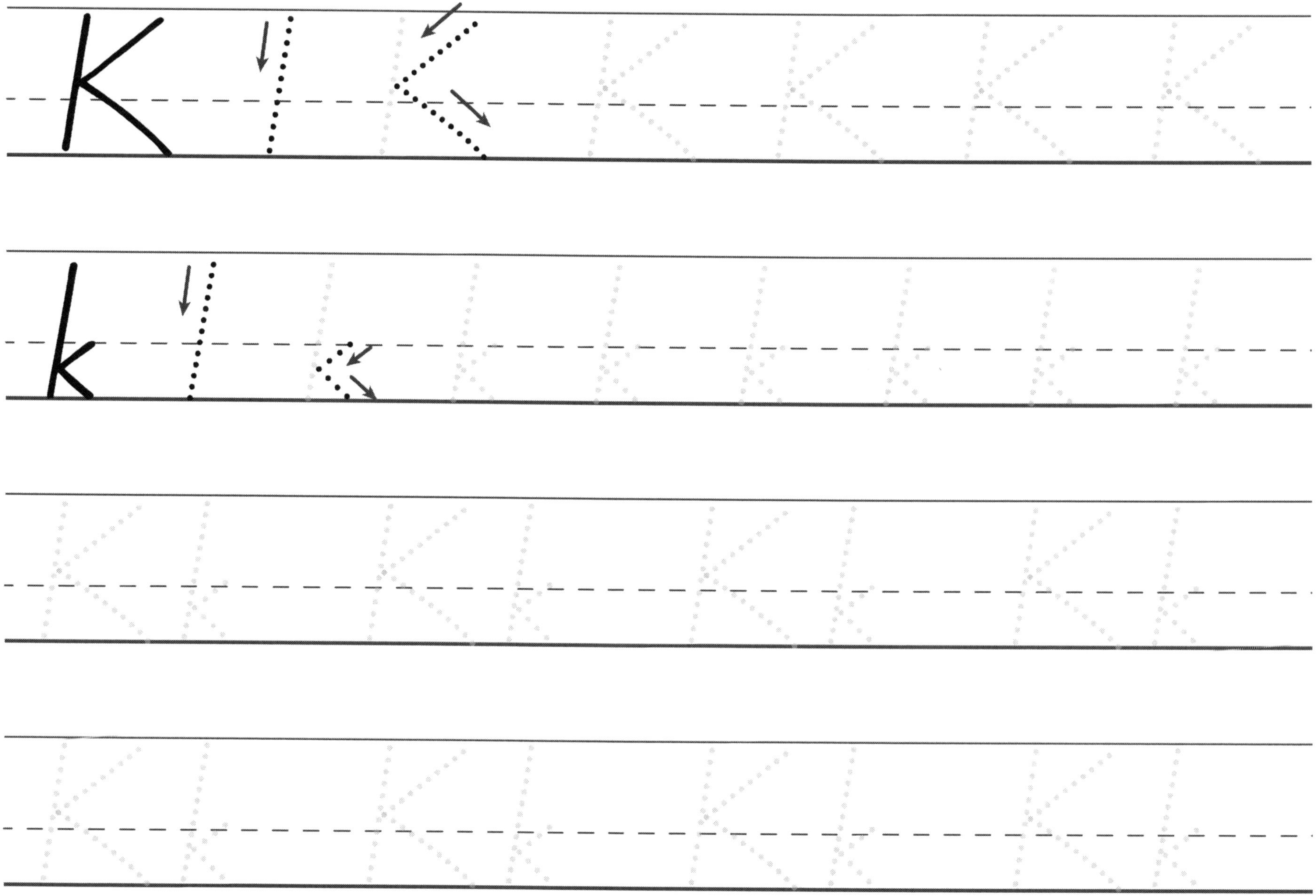

Kk

Kk

Fill in each row and complete the page with writing.

Kk

Kk

Kk

Kind

bake

walk

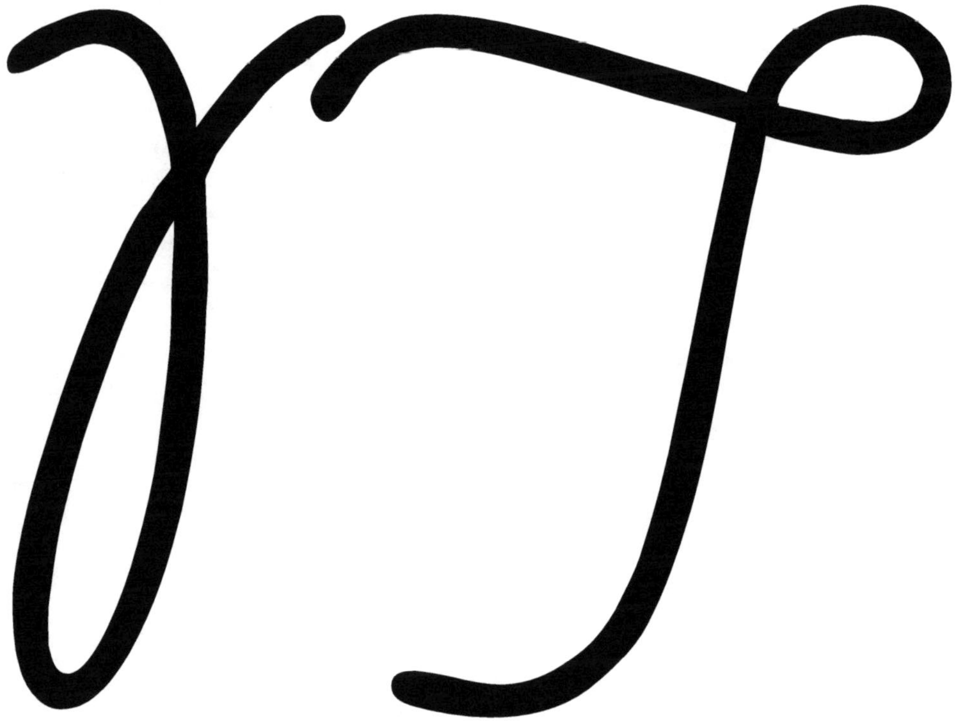

Ll

To form this letter:

L This letter begins in the upper zone just barely below the top of the upper zone and heads to the left with a curve, not an angle. At a 5-degree slant, it heads down to baseline where it comes back up with a little loop headed to the left. From the loop, the line then returns to the baseline and curves up slightly at the end. There is a sense of graceful holding in this letter.

l Beginning at the baseline, go all the way to the top of the upper zone forming a loop, then return to the baseline, reaching to the next letter with a little garland.

The letter L helps us observe our motives clearly and gain clarity in action.

This letter leads us to:
I now find Spirit in all of Life.

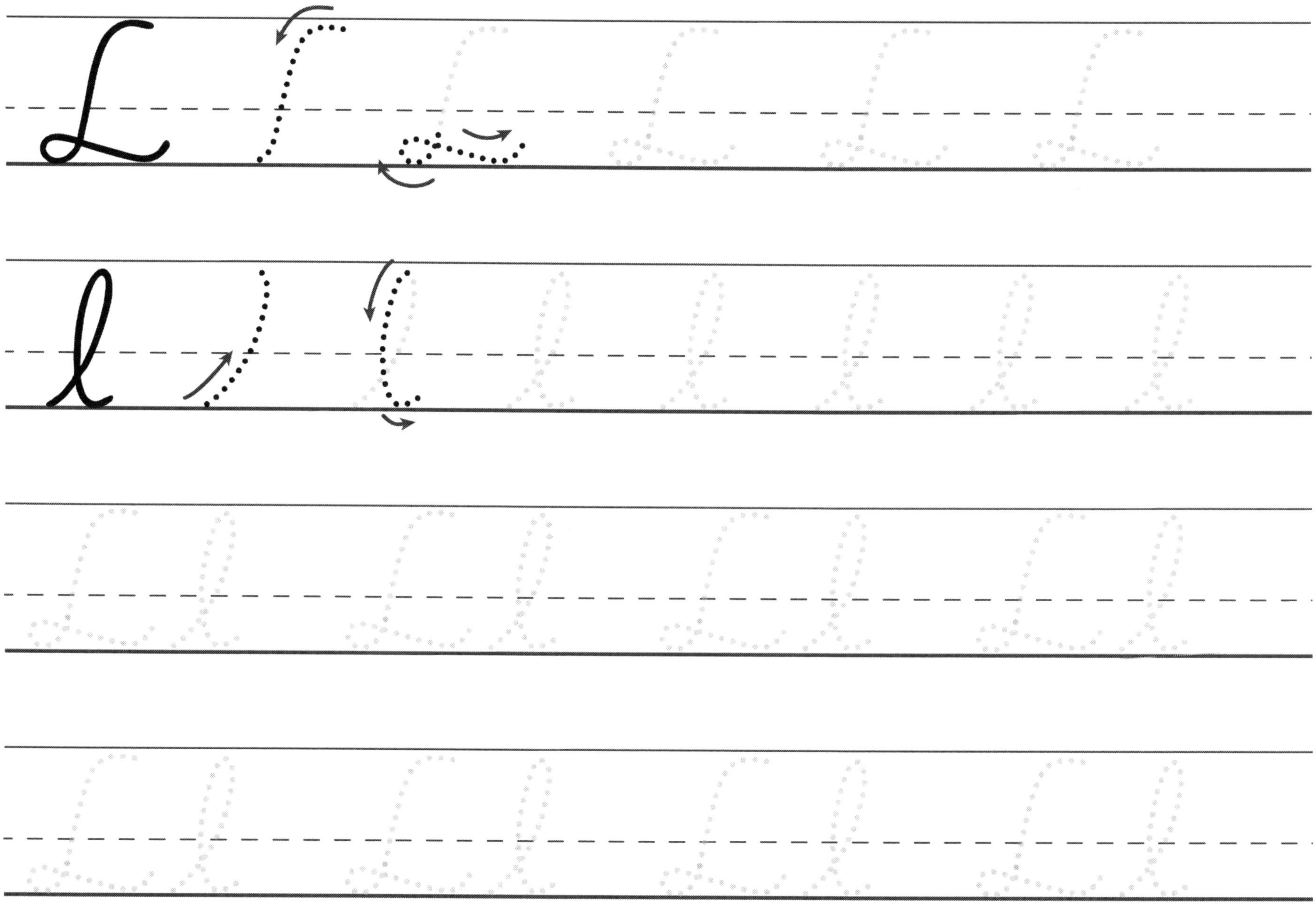

Ll

Ll

Fill in each row and complete the page with writing.

Ll

Ll

Ll

Laugh

allow

oval

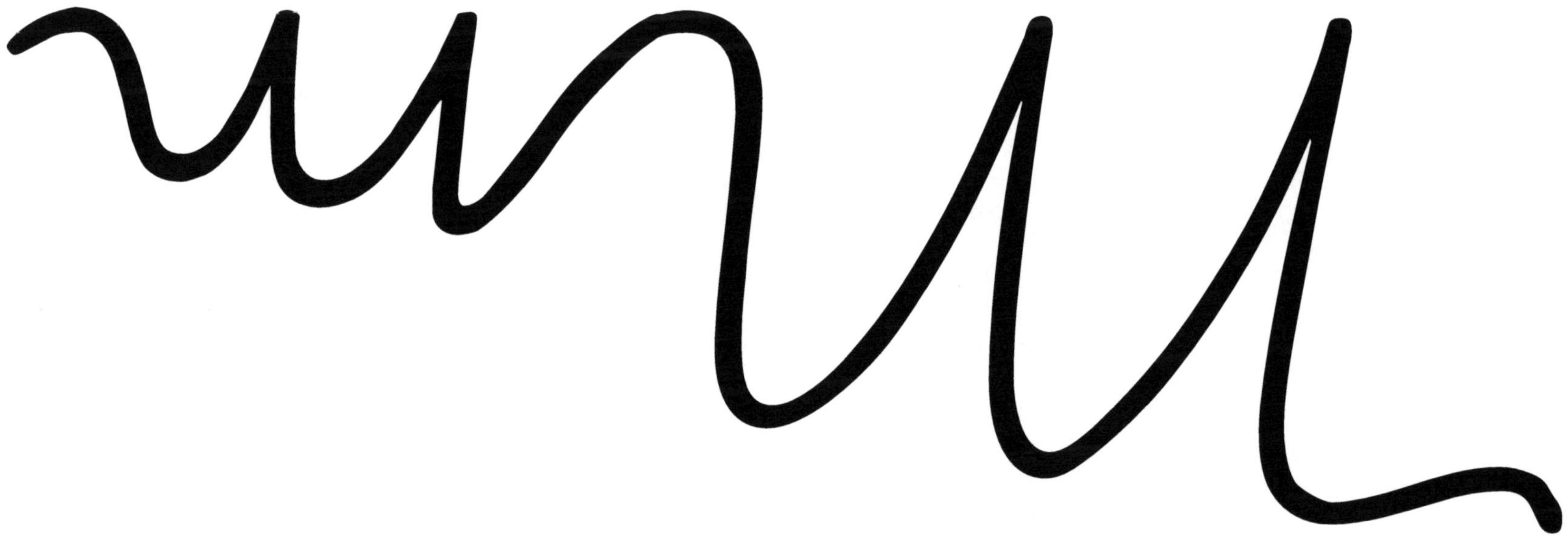

The letter M shows us our interactions with others and with Divine Grace.

This letter leads us to:
I now live in trust and surrender the need to control.

To form this letter:

M The first stroke at the top of the upper zone is a left-to-right down-scoop that forms a little cup at the top of the upper zone. Then, with a 5-degree slant, the line heads to the baseline where it makes a very narrow "v" shape before returning to the upper zone to form the second arcade. It goes back to baseline forming another narrow "v" before rising for the third arcade, which is a bit lower than the others. Returning to baseline, it reaches out with a little garland to connect to the next letter.

m Beginning at baseline, the line lifts to the top of the middle zone to form three arcades, each one successively lower. The first two arcades return to baseline with a sharp "v," but the third returns slanting slightly to the right and has a fullness before reaching to the next letter with a garland.

Mm

Mm

Fill in each row and complete the page with writing.

Mm

Mm

Mm

Many

almond

swim

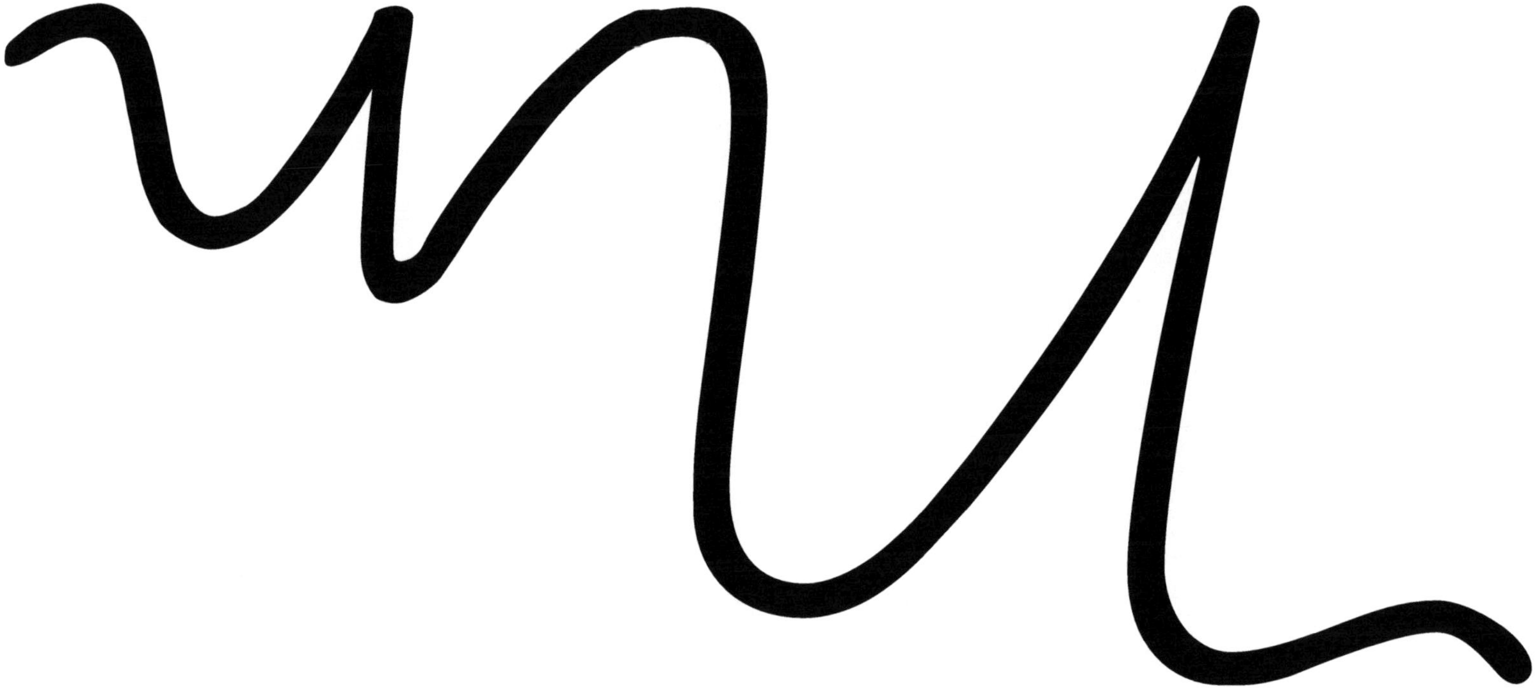

The letter N reflects the quality of our one-on-one relationships.

This letter leads us to:
I am present, playful and curious.

To form this letter:

 This letter is formed exactly like the Vimala M except there are only two arcades. The introductory stroke begins at the top of the upper zone, scoops down into a little cup filled with joyful, playful interactions, then plunges to baseline forming a sharp "v" before returning to the upper zone to form the next arcade. This arcade finishes by going straight down to baseline where it curves and reaches out with a little garland.

 Beginning at baseline, the line lifts to the top of the middle zone to form two arcades, the second one lower than the first. The first arcade returns almost straight down to baseline forming a sharp "v" before lifting again. The second arcade returns slanting slightly to the right and has a fullness before reaching baseline and extending a garland to connect with the next letter.

Nn

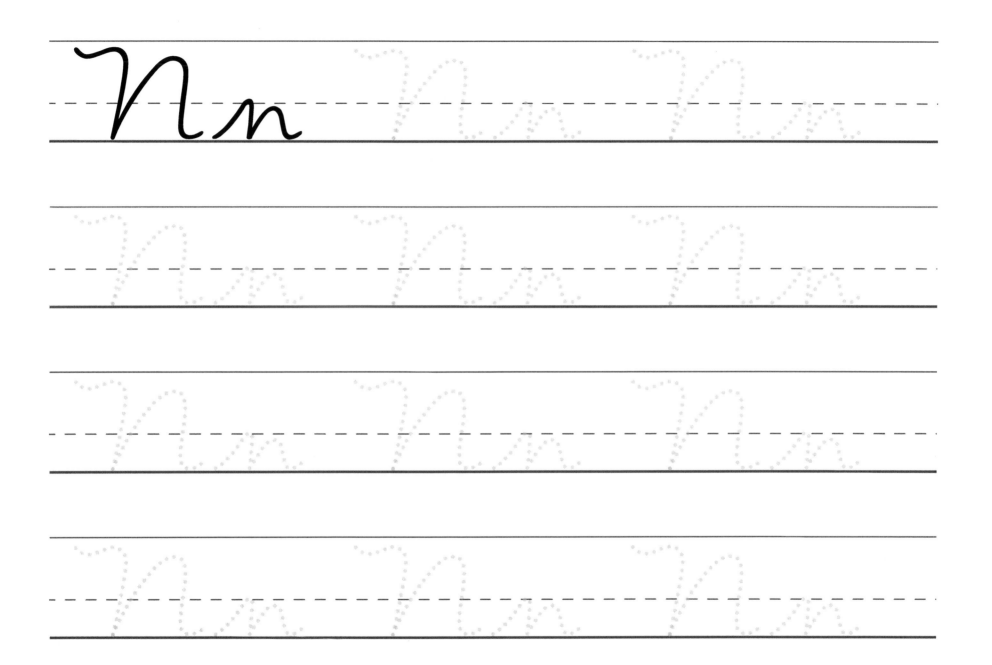

Nn

Fill in each row and complete the page with writing.

Nn

Nn

Nn

Namaste

friend

queen

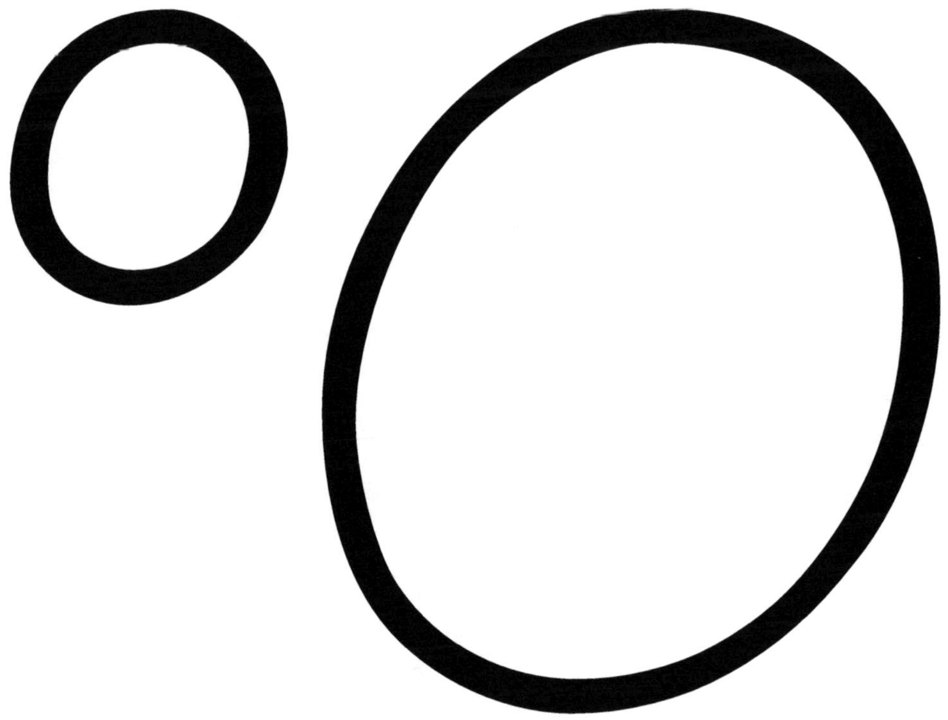

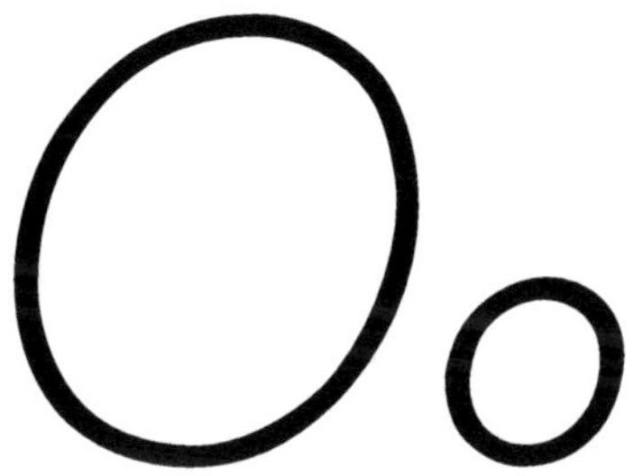

To form this letter:

O Formed clockwise, so that you end in the direction of the future, this letter is not a circle, but an oval. Starting at the top of the upper zone moving clockwise, touch the baseline before reuniting at the top to form a gentle oval.

o The lowercase letter is formed exactly the same way, except it occupies just the middle zone.

The letter O teaches communication skills, including speaking to the listener and making oneself understood.

This letter leads us to:
I speak from a sense of feeling connected to all beings and all things.

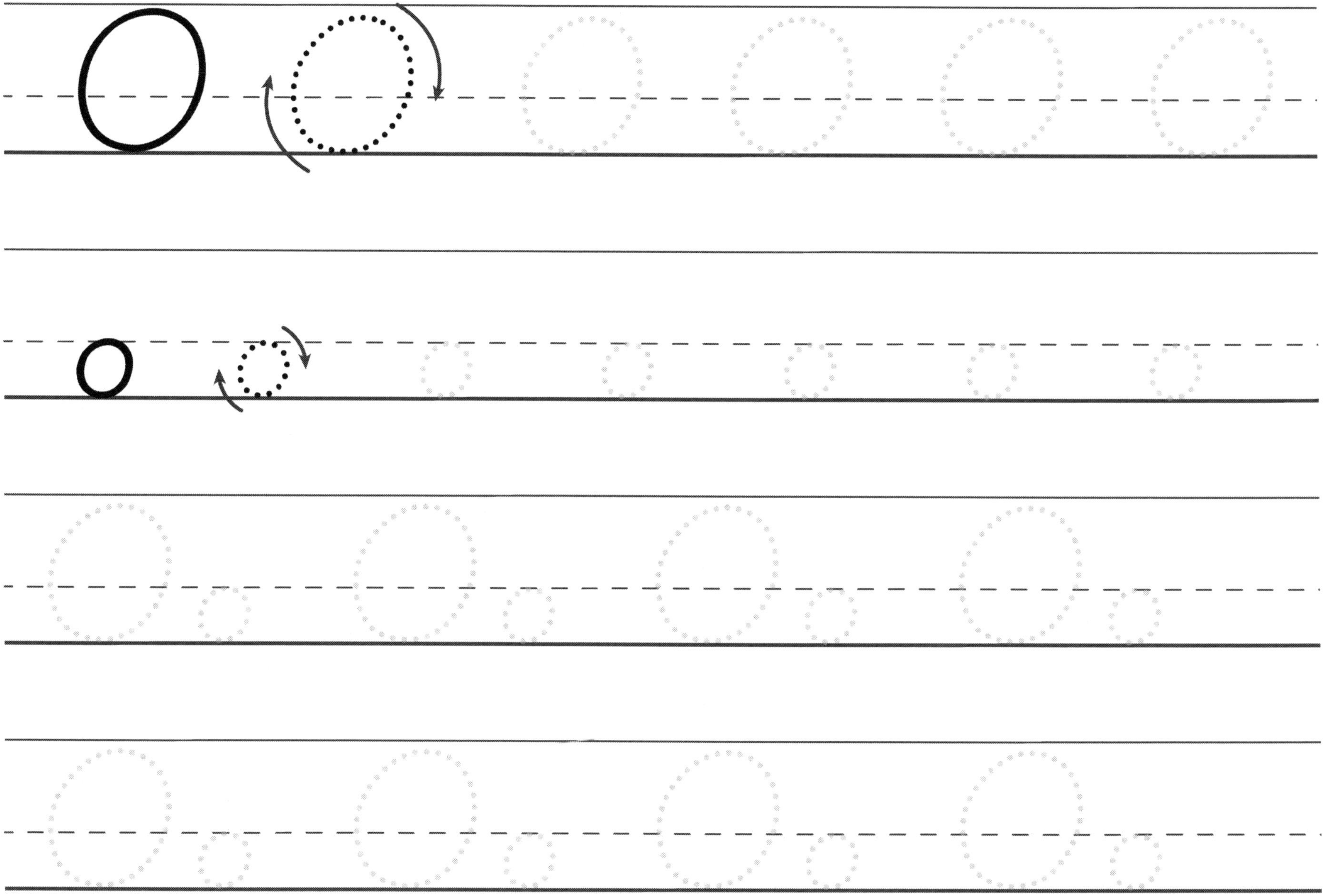

O o

Oo

Fill in each row and complete the page with writing.

Oo

Oo

Oo

Oven

positive

cheerio

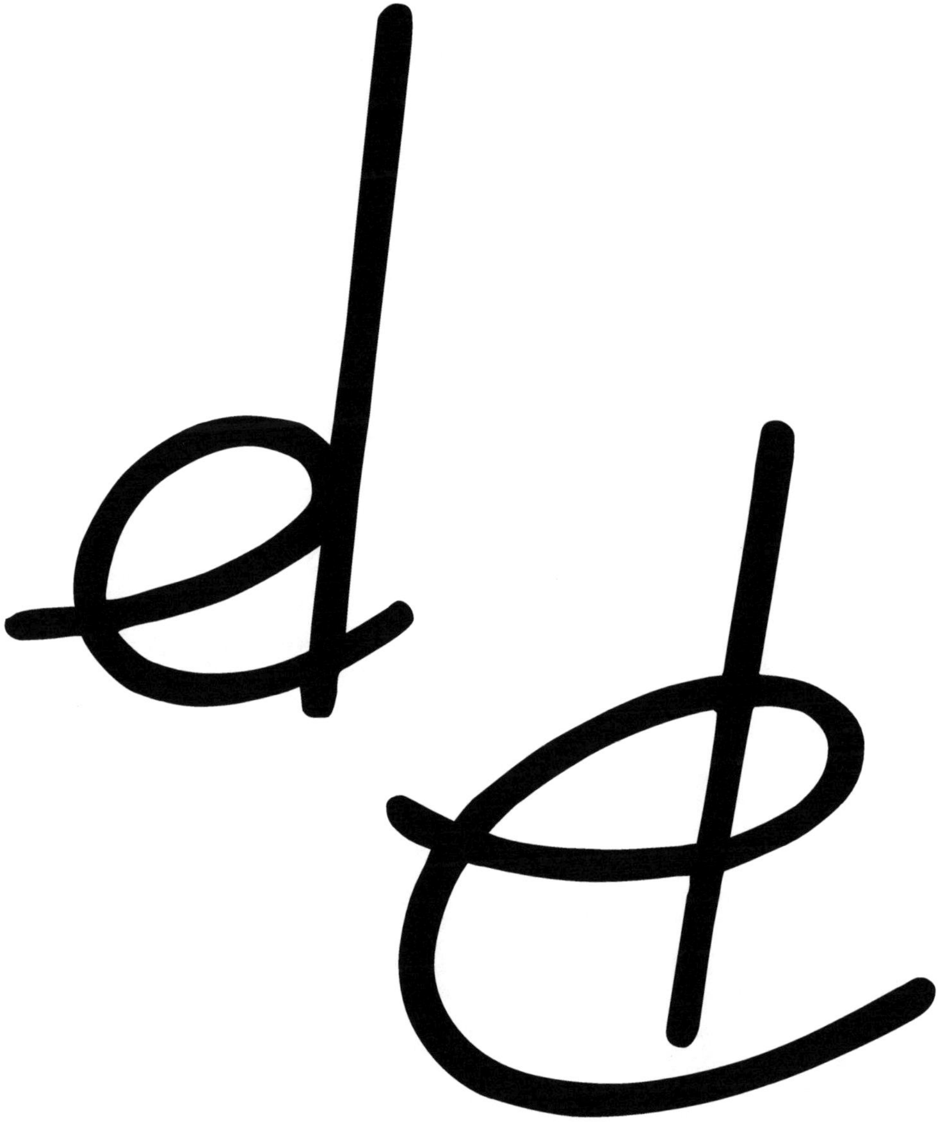

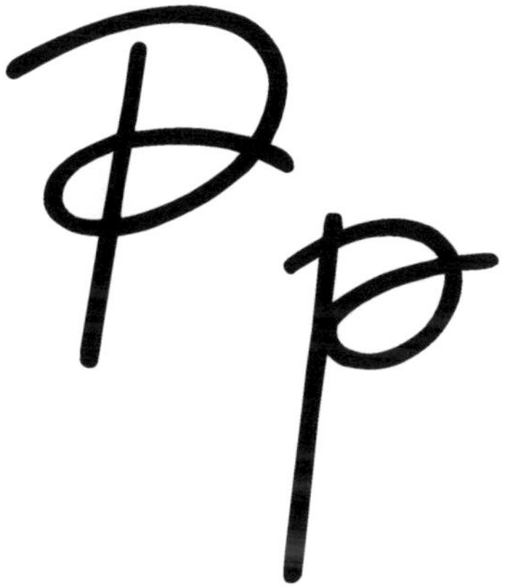

The letter P reflects our self-love and self-care.

This letter leads us to:
I love and care for myself. I am loveable, whole and complete.

To form this letter:

This letter, not surprisingly, starts with an "I am" stroke, gathering gifts from heaven for use here on earth. The second stroke starts to the left of the "I am" stroke and can either sweep slightly above it or cross it as it arcs into a backward "c" shape. When the arc returns to the "I am" stroke at the top of the middle zone, it can either cross over slightly or just touch it. Don't place too much loop to the left of the "I am" stroke. End with the prayer stroke reaching out to the top of the middle zone.

Start at the top of the middle zone and go down to the bottom of the lower zone. Lift the pen for the second stroke, a backward "c" shape that occupies only the middle zone. The ending prayer stroke reaches upward as if you were going to connect to a letter at the top of the middle zone.

Pp

Pp

Fill in each row and complete the page with writing.

Pp

Pp

Pp

People

paper

help

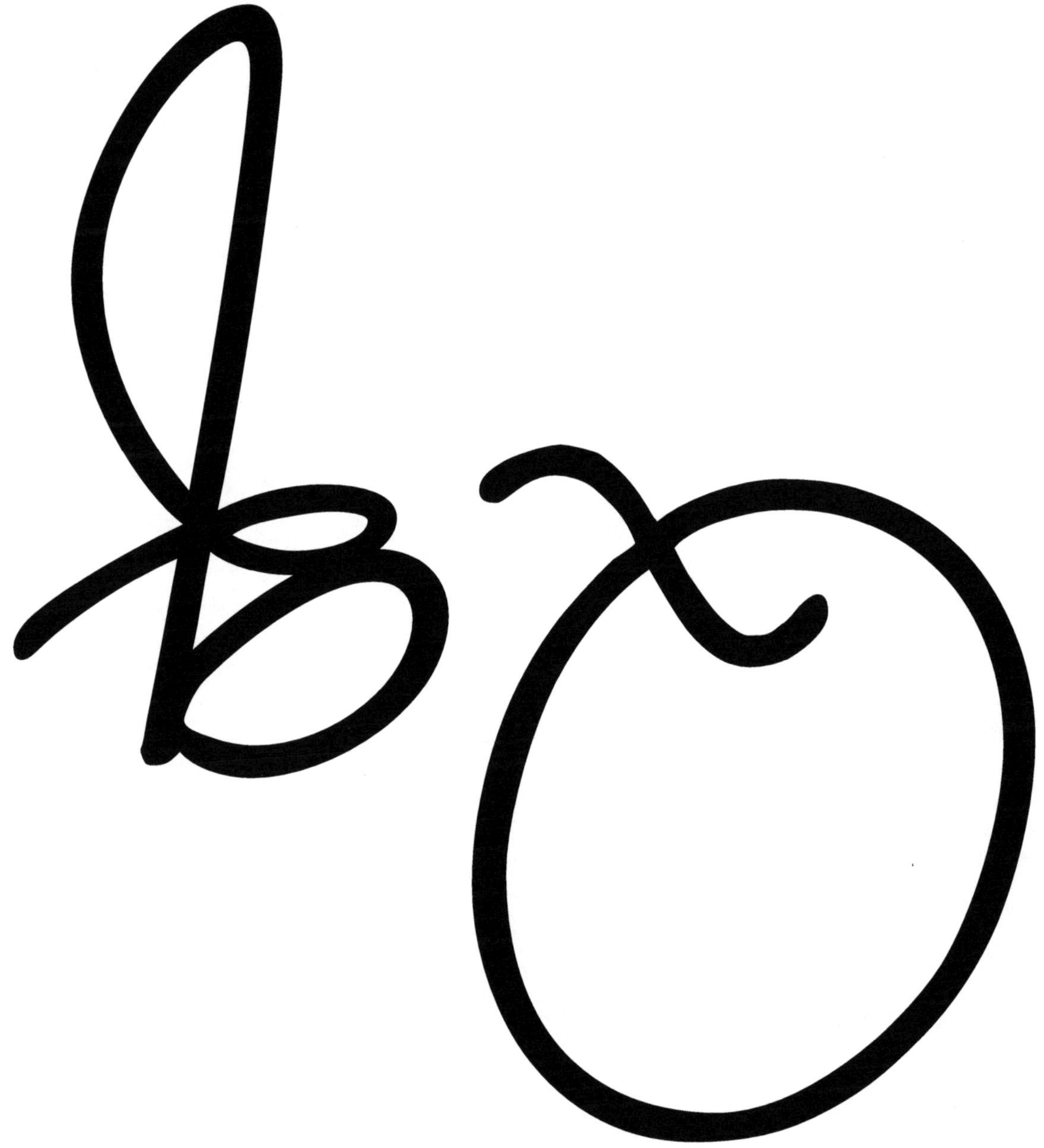

The letter Q helps us reach out to others.

This letter leads us to:
I enjoy being of service to the world.

To form this letter:

Q Starting at the top of the upper zone, form an oval in the clockwise manner as for the Vimala O. The second stroke is like the wagging tail of a dog. Starting in the lower quarter of the oval, the tail goes up and makes a curve, comes down and makes another curve. Think of a lifted-up tail wagging back and forth.

q Beginning at the top of the middle zone, form a small oval. Once it is closed, make a down stroke to the bottom of the lower zone. At the bottom, form a loop curving to the right, closing it at the baseline. Crossing left over the down stroke, make a tie stroke under the original oval—like a pillow underneath the chin of the oval. Once you have completed the tie stroke, reach upward to meet the next letter.

Qq

Qq

Fill in each row and complete the page with writing.

Qq

Qq

Qq

Query

request

Iraq

The letter R helps us generate creative insights and abilities.

This letter leads us to:
I share my creativity with others and find strength in vulnerability.

To form this letter:

R Begin with an "I am" stroke. The second stroke begins at or just left of the top of the "I am" stroke, sweeping into a backward "c" shape, quite wide, touching the "I am" stroke again about halfway down. Notice, the final stroke reaching to the right touches the baseline beyond the belly of the backward "c" shape above.

r Start at baseline, come to the top of the middle zone, form a small loop, then dip down and back up, making a point at the top of the middle zone. Then drop to the baseline and reach forward with a garland.

r For this alternative lowercase r, begin as shown, forming the first arcade. Return to the top of the middle zone with a partial arcade that reaches higher than the first and ends at the top of the middle zone. From this point, do not connect to the next letter. The pen is lifted before the next letter begins.

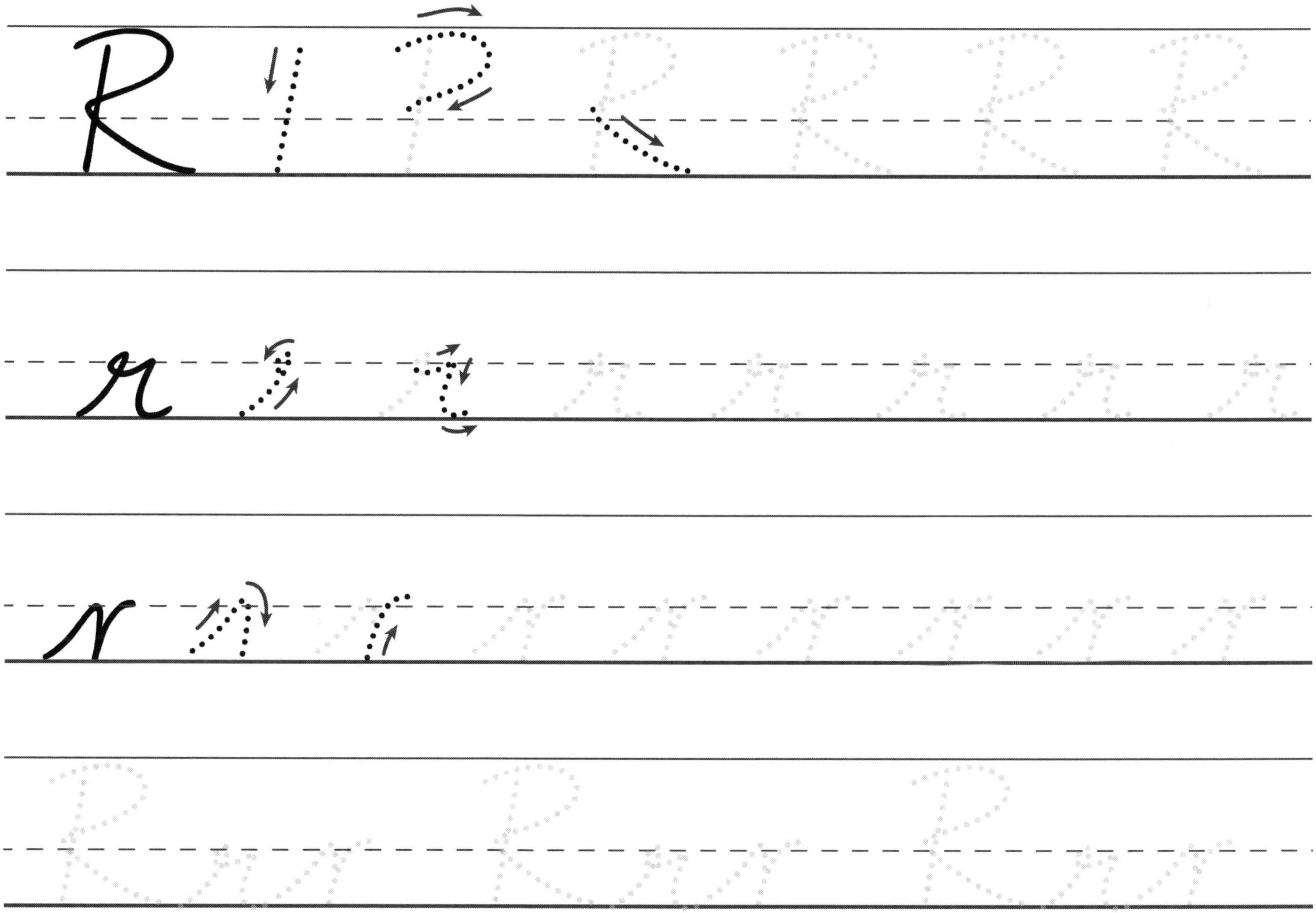

Rrr

Rr

Fill in each row and complete the page with writing.

Rr

Rr

Rr

Resolve

syrup

advisor

To form this letter:

S Starting in the upper zone, form two "c" shapes. The first is forward-facing, the second backward-facing. Once you have finished the second backward "c" shape, reach forward with the prayer stroke heading toward the top of the middle zone. There are no angles in this letter, it is smooth and flowing. The 5-degree slant can be seen on the outer left edges of the form.

s The lowercase letter is formed like the uppercase, except it occupies only the middle zone.

The letter S represents the continuum of balance.

This letter leads us to:
I now have balance and awareness of my degree of balance.

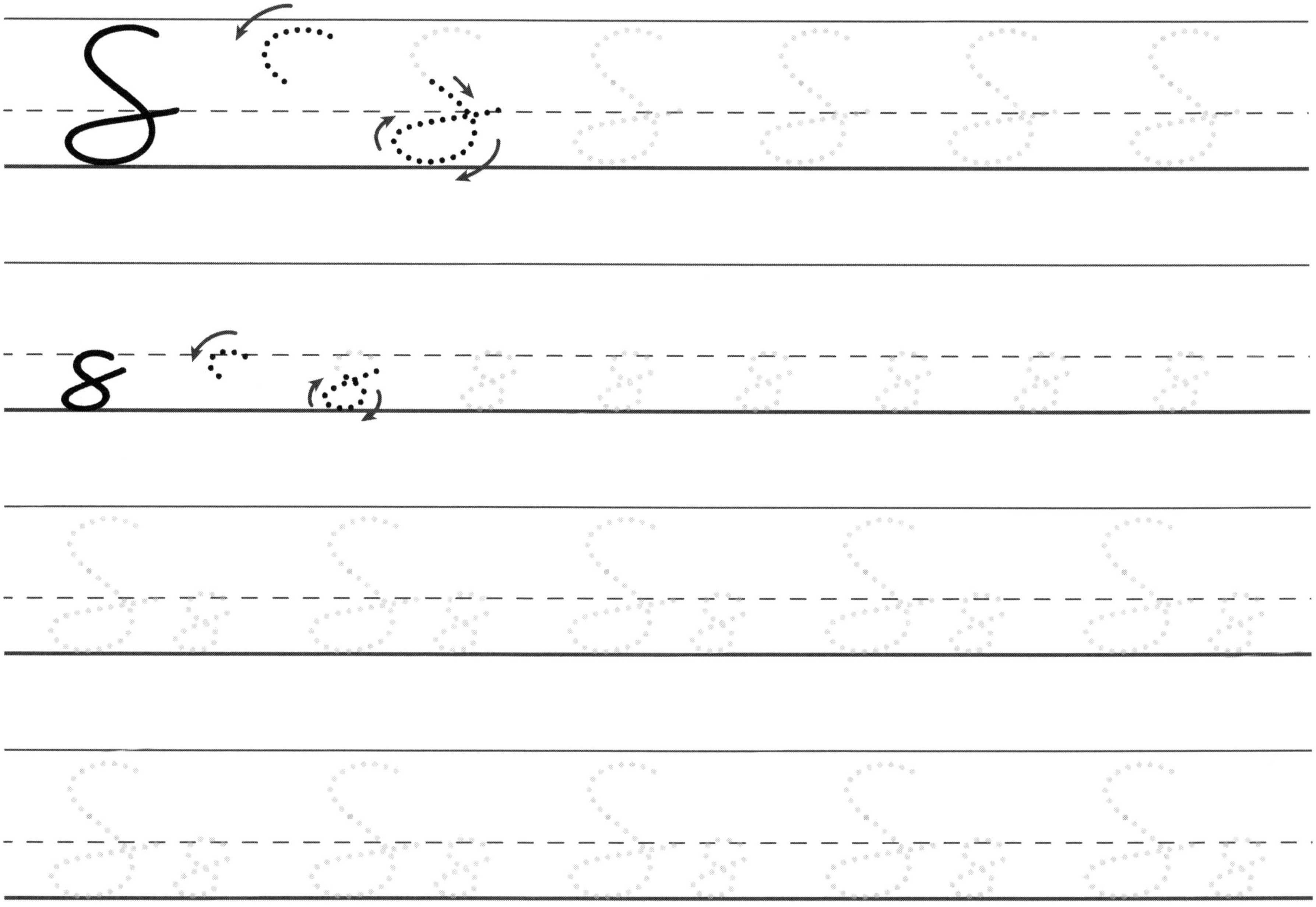

Ss

S s

Fill in each row and complete the page with writing.

Ss

Ss

Ss

Smile

also

iris

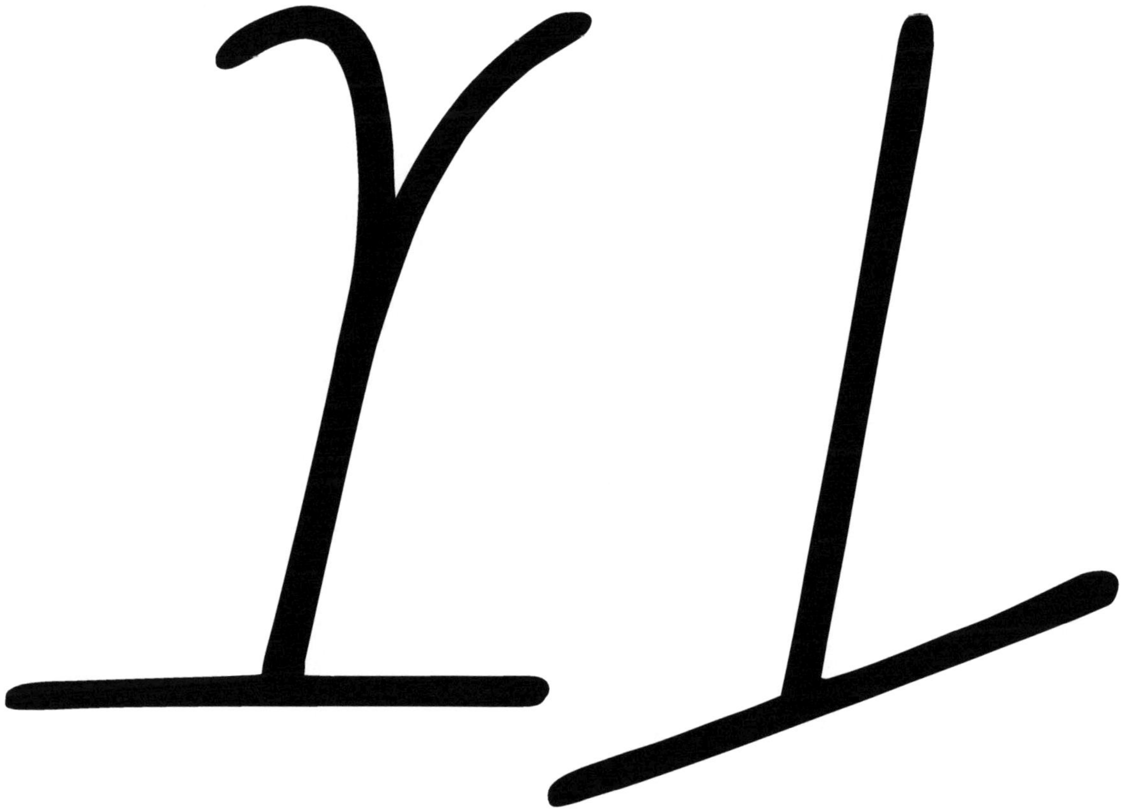

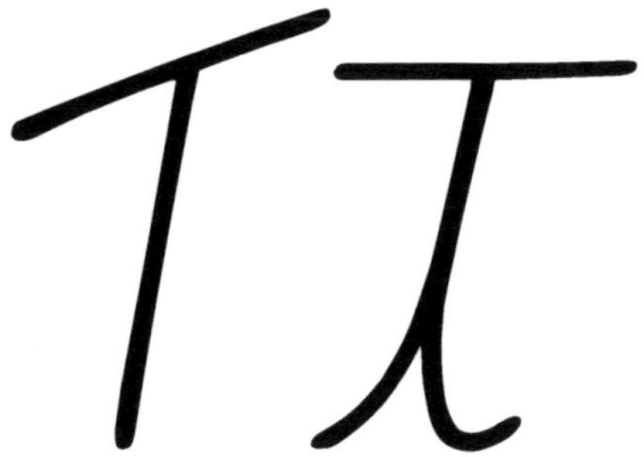

The letter T speaks to one's role in life.

This letter leads us to:
I find my work and I do it well.

To form this letter:

Begin with an "I am" stroke and then form a top crossbar from left to right, making sure the right side is elevated. It is important to have the crossbar centered evenly on both sides of the stem. This balances the left, representing the past, and the right, which represents the future.

Begin at baseline and reach to the top of the upper zone. From there, the upstroke is retraced back down to the middle zone where it separates, forming a small inverted "v" in the middle zone before reaching forward with a small garland at baseline. There are no loops. Add a crossbar going straight across from left to right, again balancing past and future by centering it evenly on the stem.

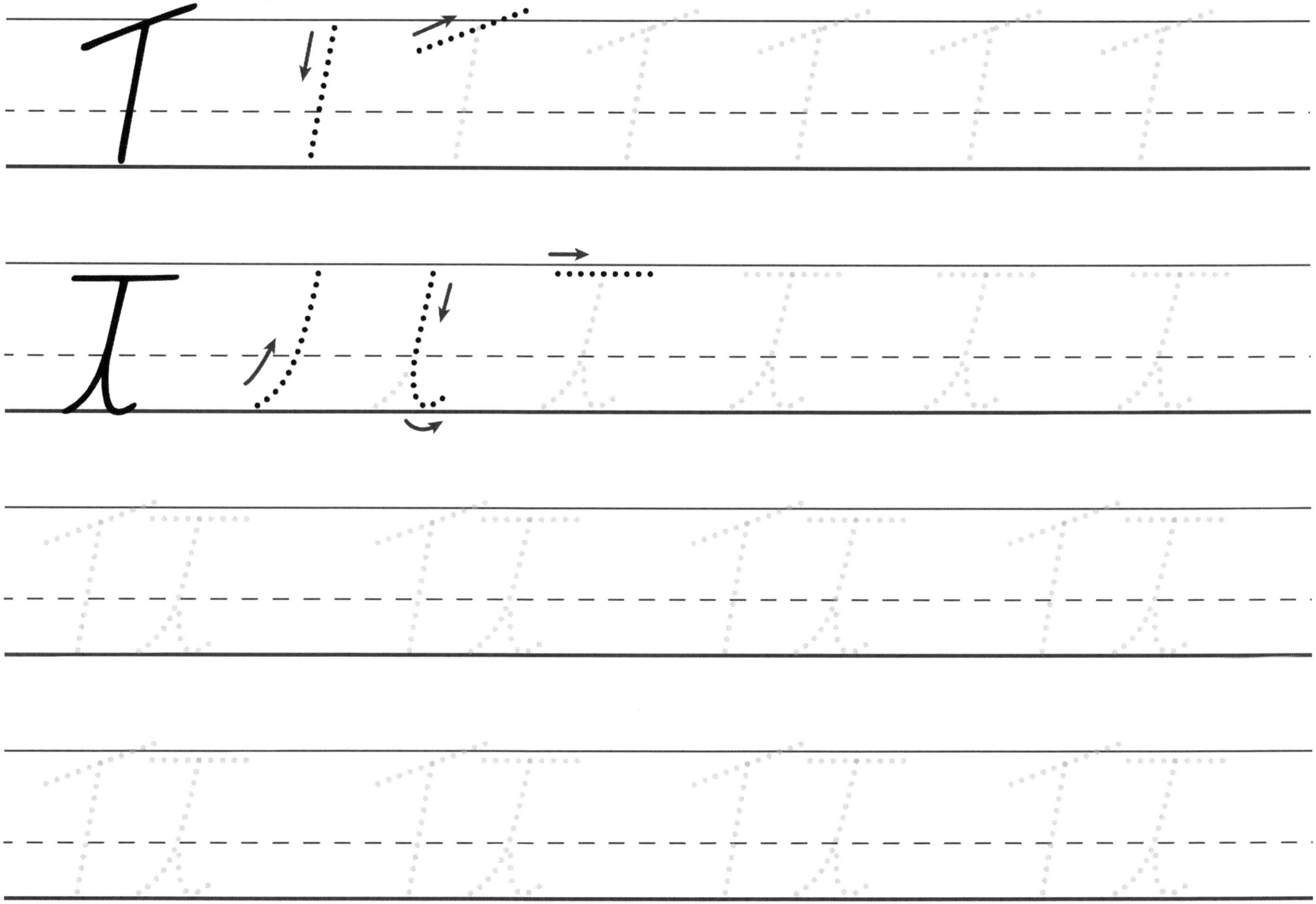

Ππ

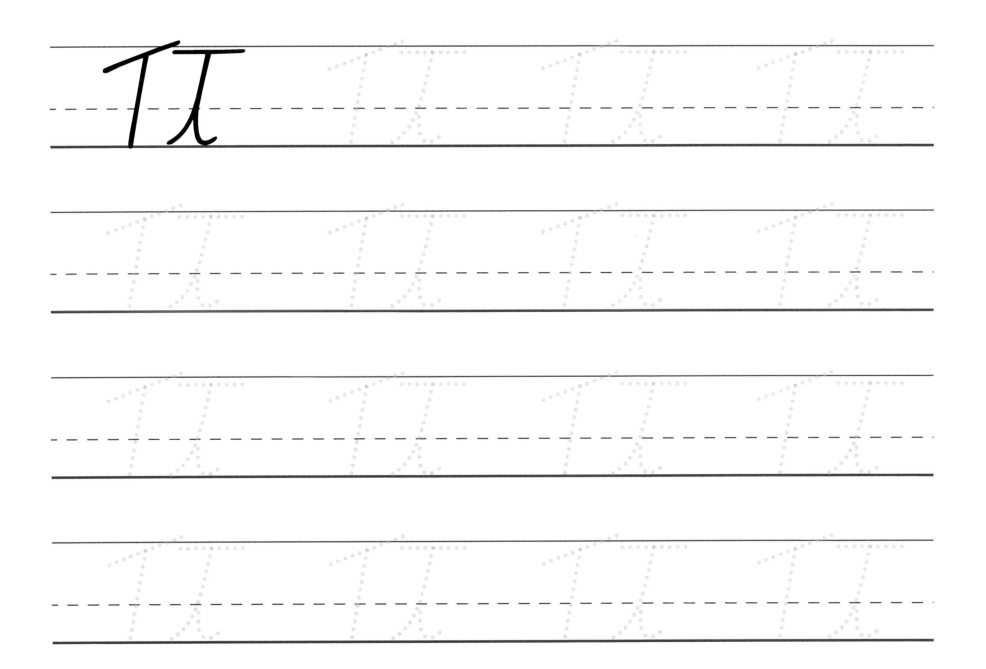

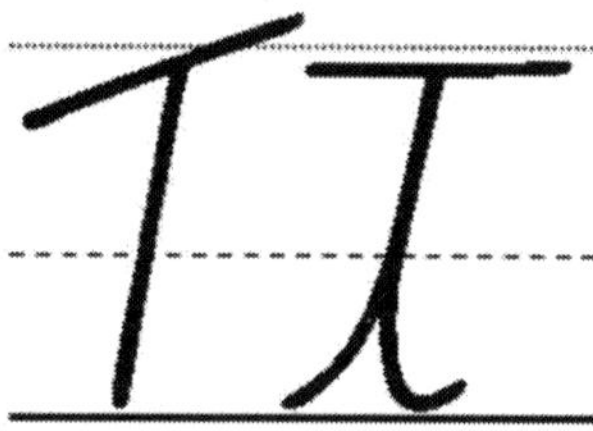

Fill in each row and complete the page with writing.

T t

T t

T t

Tame

attend

benefit

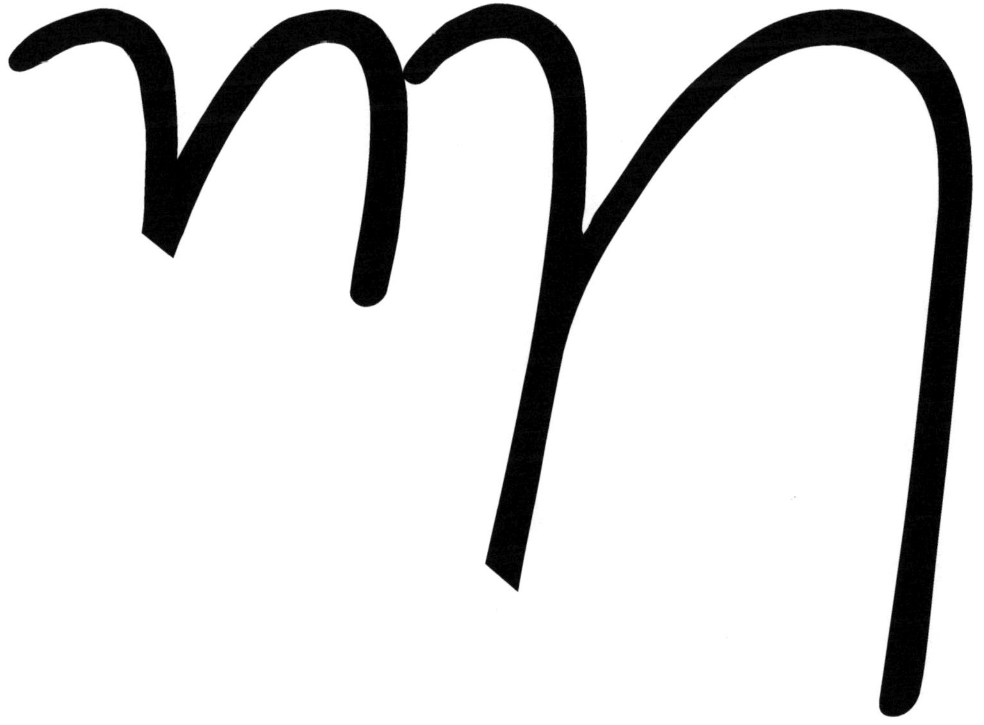

To form this letter:

U Start at the very top of the upper zone and come down to baseline at a 5-degree slant. The left side of the letter forms a garland before it hits baseline, sweeping upward into the right side, forming a smooth cup with straight sides. The right side is slightly lower than the left, so that your cup of gifts "pours" toward the future. From here, the line retraces itself back down to baseline where it curves to reach out to the next letter with a small garland.

u The lowercase letter begins at the top of the middle zone, occupying only the middle zone; otherwise is formed identically.

The letter U teaches us openness.

This letter leads us to:
I am open to new ideas and ways of doing things.

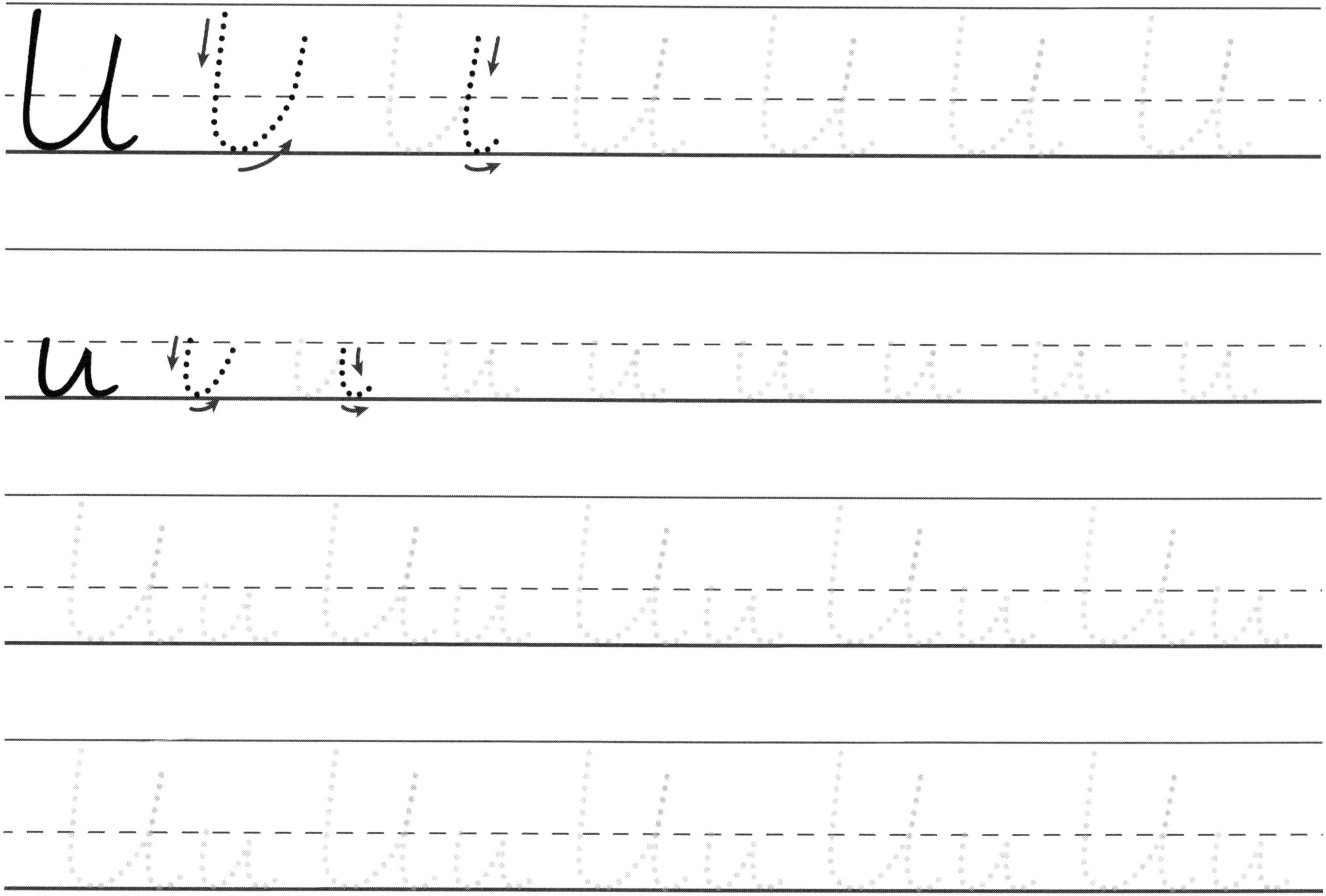

Uu

Uu

Fill in each row and complete the page with writing.

Uu

Uu

Uu

Under

found

haiku

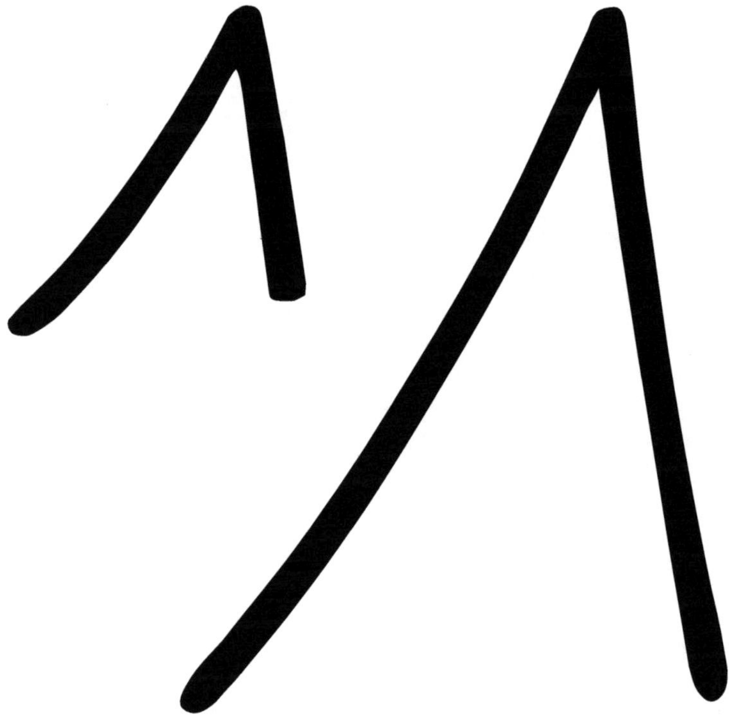

To form this letter:

V This letter begins just barely below the top of the upper zone, angles to the baseline, forms a point, and returns to the very top of the upper zone. The form speaks to decisiveness. Both lines are almost straight, there are no garlands, and the letter, at the baseline, is a single point. The right arm is slightly longer, giving this letter the mood of a checkmark.

v Proceed as previously described only start just under the top of the middle zone.

The letter V represents discernment and clarity in decision making.

This letter leads us to:
I consider the impact of my actions and decisions and move accordingly.

Vv

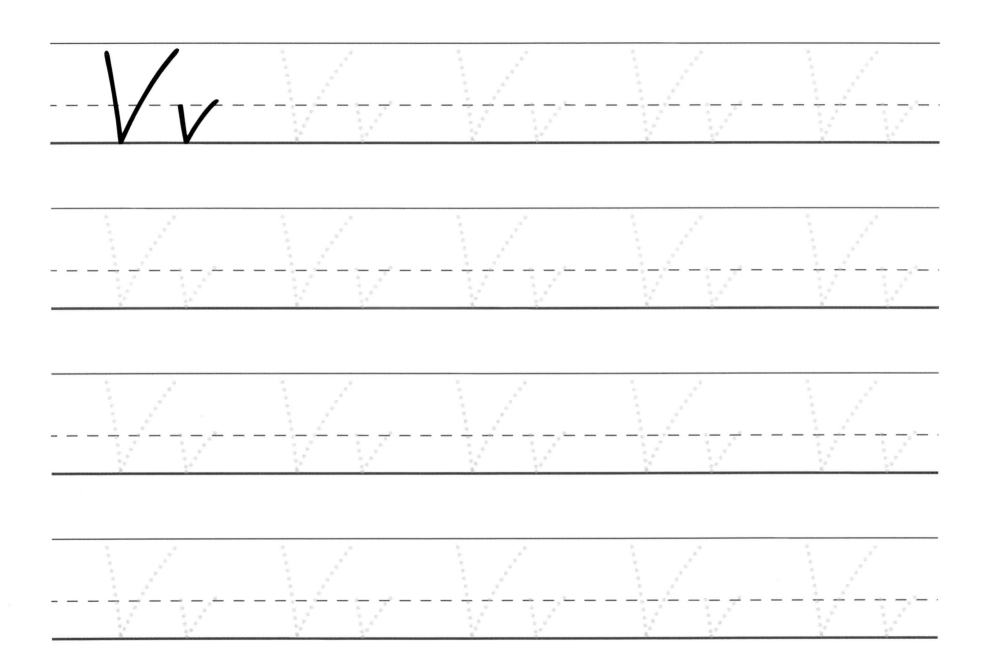

Vv

Fill in each row and complete the page with writing.

Vv

Vv

Vv

Vision

love

improv

Ww

To form this letter:

W Beginning at the top of the upper zone, head down in a gently curved line to baseline, form a garland and curve back up to the upper zone, ending slightly lower than you started. From here, return to baseline, make another garland, and head back to the upper zone. The height of the final upstroke is taller than the middle stroke, but shorter than the beginning stroke (so the receiving and sharing cups can mix and also flow outward).

w Starting at the top of the middle zone, gently curve to baseline in a garland, go back up to the top of the middle zone, then drop back down to baseline forming another garland and return to the top of the middle zone. The letter can end by reaching out with a bridge stroke just below the top of the middle zone.

The letter W is the letter of the teacher. It represents openness to receive (the first cup) and openness to share (the second cup).

This letter leads us to:
I love to learn and I share my skills lovingly.

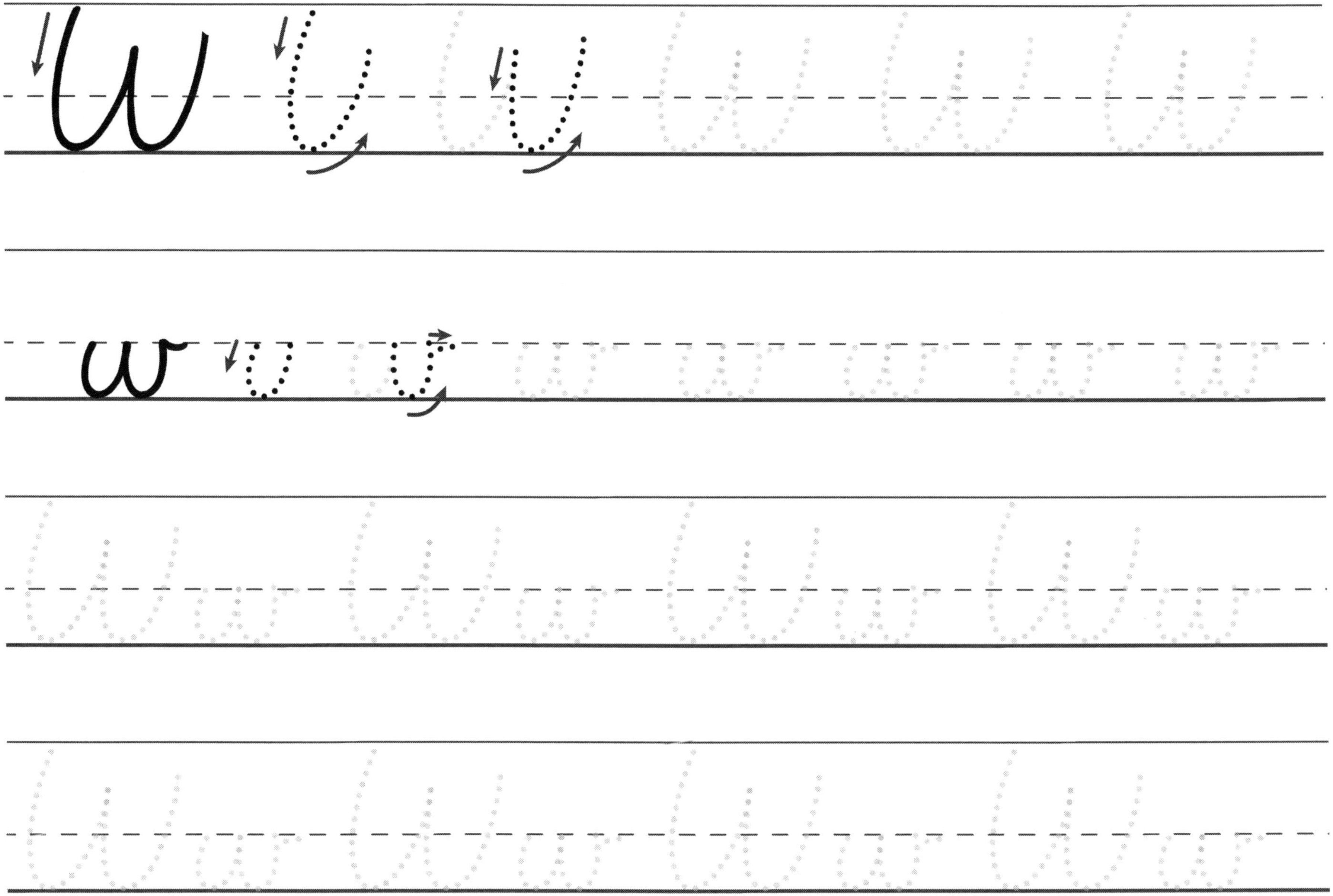

Ww

Ww

Fill in each row and complete the page with writing.

Ww

Ww

Ww

Work

sweet

renew

xX

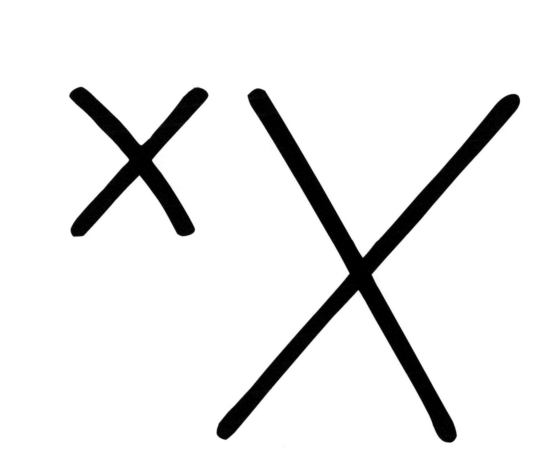

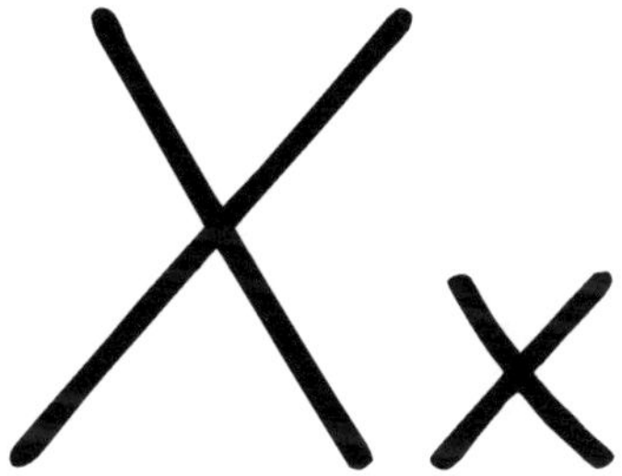

To form this letter:

X The first stroke begins at the top of the upper zone and heads left to the baseline. The second stroke begins to the left of the first stroke, and ends at the baseline on the right. Like a healthy inner authority, this letter is never connected or "propped up" on either side, it always stands alone. Notice that this letter is composed of "v" shapes that intersect at the heart ("v" representing discernment and decision making). It is important that the heart of this letter be at the center of the form.

x The lowercase letter is crafted identically, only it stays completely within the middle zone.

The letter X represents inner authority.

This letter leads us to:
I follow my inner guidance, bringing clarity and ease to my life and situations.

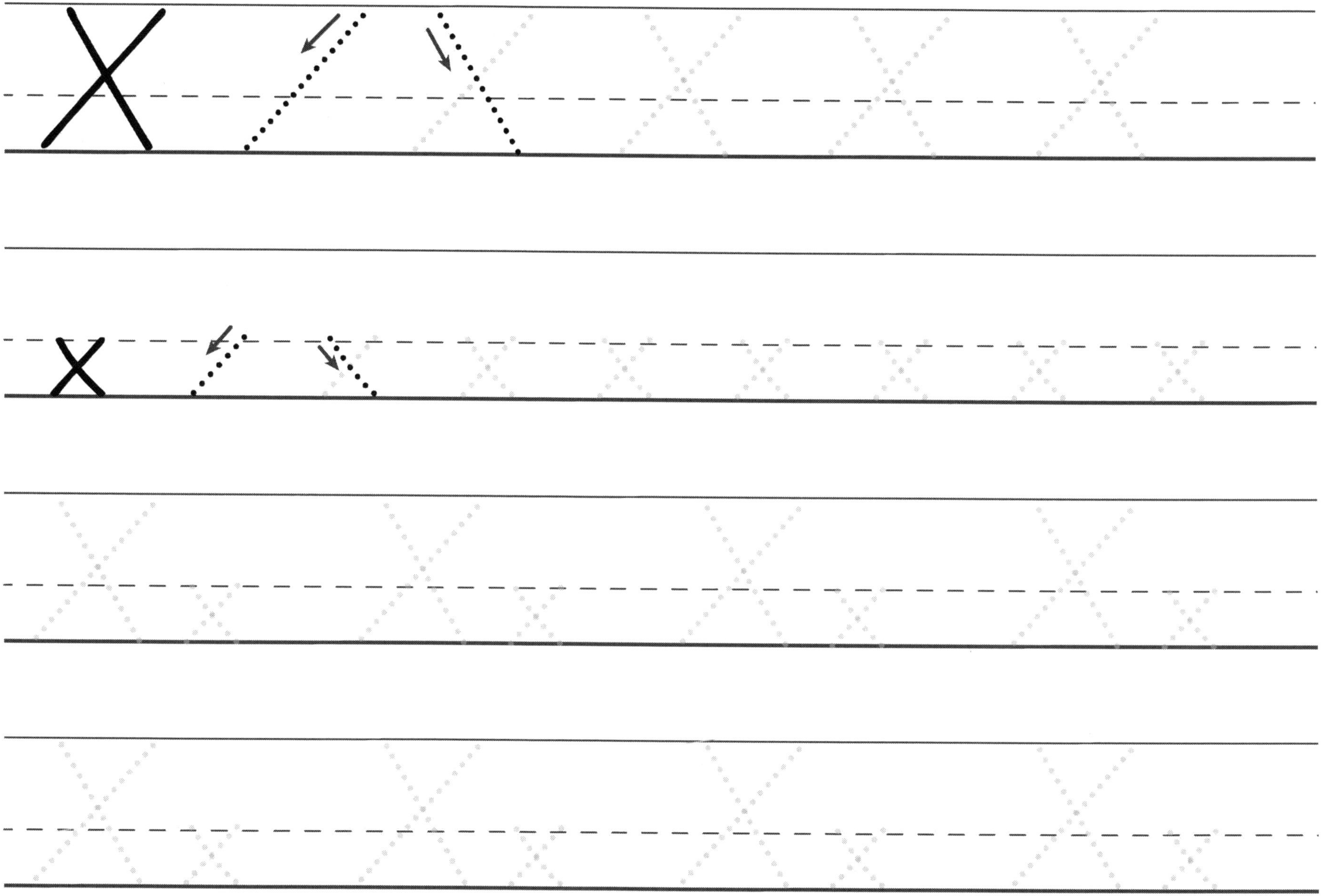

X x

Xx

Fill in each row and complete the page with writing.

Xx

Xx

Xx

Xena

Taxi

mix

h h

To form this letter:

Y This letter starts like the uppercase Vimala U, holding openness and understanding. From here, the letter dives straight down to the lower zone and forms a loop capturing the perseverance and determination that live in the lower zone. The letter returns to the middle zone and ends in the middle zone.

y The lowercase letter is exactly the same as the uppercase except the "u" shape only occupies the middle zone. Notice that the loop that dives into the lower zone is a bit smaller to keep the letter in balance.

The letter Y teaches self-worth and the value of our contribution.

This letter leads us to:
I am both humble and self-respecting and know the honest value of what I contribute.

Yy

Yy

Fill in each row and complete the page with writing.

Yy

Yy

Yy

Yes

style

cozy

E E

To form this letter:

 Start slightly below the top of the upper zone with a backward "c" shape, finishing near the top of the middle zone. From here, the letter reaches out into another backward "c" shape, only this one is much longer, descending through the middle zone and into the lower zone, creating a lower loop that returns and closes in the middle zone. Finishing the loop in the middle zone is essential to capture the lower zone energy.

 Formed exactly like its uppercase counterpart, this letter begins near the top of the middle zone and ends near the bottom the middle zone.

The letter Z helps us to accept life as it really is.

This letter leads us to:
I feel a deep contentment with life.

Zz

Zz

Fill in each row and complete the page with writing.

Zz

Zz

Zz

Zoo

hazel

waltz

Index of Human Qualities and The Corresponding Letter

I recommend working on no more than three letters at any given time, sticking with them until mastery. The amount of time needed to do this can vary considerably, but be sure to practice each letter for at least a 40-day cycle. Some letters may require multiple cycles but do not despair, the harder the letter is to master, the more benefit will come to you. It is difficult because you are creating new neurological pathways that will bring change into your life.

To choose your letters, begin by relaxing into non-performance mode and write a full page in your natural handwriting on what you would like to be different in your life. It is important to do this on plain unlined paper. Date and save this writing so you have a point of reference.

In reviewing your writing, I look at many things in addition to the letters themselves, such as slant, baseline, spacing and margins. In choosing someone's practice letters, I look for:

- Letters that sometimes, but not always, are similar to the Vimala letters. These letters generally indicate qualities you are nearing mastery of, but need a small nudge. It's a good place to begin.
- Letters that block the things you desire. For example, if you wish to have more friends and reach out to others, look at the N and Q. The list of human qualities can help you select letters that will give you the most support.
- Forms that universally block positive development. In Part Four of my book, *Soul Development through Handwriting*, I give examples of undesirable forms.

Once a letter is mastered, add a new one so you are always working on three letters. Trying to do more than three letters at once just leads to overwhelm. To select your new letter, write another handwritten page of what you would like to be different about your life.

Enjoy the dance and watch your life take on a new level of mastery along with the letters!

Book Reference Key: s *Soul Development through Handwriting: The Waldorf Approach to the Vimala Alphabet®* by Jennifer Crebbin
d *How the Letters Dance Me* by Jennifer Crebbin

		Page
Acceptance of life	Letter Z	159d
Acceptance of others	Letter E	33d
Ambition	Letter T	57s
Authority, attitude toward	Letter K	47s
	Margins	24s
Authority, personal	Letter K	47s
	Letter X	61s, 147d
Balance	Letter S	56s, 117d
	Line slant	26s
Being present	Letter I	35s
Boundaries	Letter D	41s
Clarity in actions, motives	Letter L	75d
Clear seeing	Letter I	57d
Codependency	Letter P	53s
Communication, verbal	Letter O	93
Communication, written	Letter E	34s
Community	Letter B	39s
Compassion	Letter E	34s
Compassionate speech	Letter O	36s

		Page
Completion	Letter G	45d
	Tie strokes	28s
Confidence	Letter A	9d
	Letter H	51d
	Letter X	61s
Conflict/Confrontation	Letter D	41s
Contentment	Letter Z	63s, 159d
Control, need for	Letter T, Crossbar	no reference
Creativity	Letter F	42s, 39d
	Letter R	55s, 111d
Discernment, decisions	Letter V	59s, 135d
Disorganization	Line spacing	27s
Divine Grace	Letter M	50s, 81d
Escapism	Letter L	49s
Focus	Letter G	45d
Generosity	Letter B	15d
Gratitude	Letter G	44s, 45d
Grounding	Baseline	24s
Intuition, insight	Letter J	46s, 63d

Made in United States
Troutdale, OR
10/05/2023

13436463R00097